Martin Lloyd Williams is married to  children. He is rector of St Michael's and honorary chaplain to Bath Men

BEAUTY AND BROKENNESS

BEAUTY AND BROKENNESS

Compassion and the Kingdom of God

Martin Lloyd Williams

First published in Great Britain in 2007

Society for Promoting Christian Knowledge
36 Causton Street
London SW1P 4ST

Copyright © Martin Lloyd Williams 2007

British Library Cataloguing-in-Publication Data
A catalogue record for this book is available from the British Library

ISBN 978–0–281–05858–7

1 3 5 7 9 10 8 6 4 2

Typeset by Graphicraft Ltd, Hong Kong
Printed in the UK by CPI Bookmarque, Croydon, CR0 4TD

For Jackie,
Tegan, Benedict and Holly

Contents

Foreword by Professor Frances Young	xi
Preface	xv
1 So many questions	1
2 Is God really disabled?	17
3 Beauty, blessing and boundaries	33
4 Which way now?	55
5 So what's new?	75
6 Compassion	101
7 Fulfilling our vocation to compassion	117
Notes	135

Foreword

When you have been on a journey yourself it is always good to meet someone who has travelled the same way. Here I gladly greet a companion who has seen some of the same views, shared like perspectives, enjoyed similar discoveries and loved identical beauty spots, as well as surviving comparable struggles and hurts. Metaphor that may be, and an extended one at that, but it describes something like what this book has meant to me. Our questions and interests diverge somewhat, yet overlap; through comparable experiences we have been endowed with similar treasures and parallel insights, and it has been refreshing to pursue this alternative route to much the same destination. Reading this book has been deeply humbling: its wisdom appears so matter-of-fact, whereas for me insight never came that easily; indeed, it took some dozen years in the wilderness of doubt before I began to discern that I had privileged access to the deepest truths of Christianity – to the beauty and brokenness at the heart of the faith.

This is a work of reflection and theological enquiry rather than anecdotal or autobiographical narrative, though stories punctuate it and it is always in the light of disability, both congenital and acquired, that we are invited to look again at the great doctrines of incarnation, fall and redemption, creation and re-creation, as well as human nature and the vocation of disciples of Jesus Christ. The challenging circumstances that generated this reflection are outlined in the Preface; actual experiences earth the thinking in concrete, physical realities. Sometimes through art and literature, often through the Bible, occasionally in other ways, we are challenged to see things in dramatically new ways: What if 'God wanted to become human so badly that he would go to the extent of accepting disability in order to become human'? Suppose we were to take seriously, as did St Francis of Assisi, God's identification with the marginalized and the wounding of Christ's body on the cross? Are we not 'all incomplete works in progress', God being 'at work turning us inside out both for his glory and for our growth into maturity'? Shouldn't we have 'in our minds the image of a disabled body as being an appropriate and normative image for the Church rather than an able-bodied image'?

But in the title 'Beauty' appears before 'Brokenness', and that proves significant. We are told that Genesis 1 has God declaring that creation is good – aesthetically good rather than morally good! – and that John's Gospel speaks of the 'Beautiful Shepherd' if we look closely at the original Greek. Beauty enriches our lives, but convention determines too much what we see as beautiful. 'To spend any time at all in the company of those who have disabilities is to discover to our shame that beauty, like God himself, is not always where we thought it was.' Blessing, like beauty, is received from welcoming those who are different, and crossing boundaries.

'[T]he beauty of God pours out of us through the cracks in our lives' – that's how the book ends. It begins with reflection on the cover picture, Andreas Mantegna's *Presentation of Christ in the Temple*, painted around 1465. The possibility is that the artist depicted Jesus as a boy with Down's syndrome. This profoundly challenging idea reminds me of a moment of deep significance in my own journey.

It was 1991, the 20th anniversary pilgrimage of Faith and Light, a sister organization to the L'Arche communities.* Some 20,000 people from all over the world were gathered in the piazza before the great basilica at Lourdes. It was the closing ceremony on Easter Monday. The story of Mary coming to the tomb was told over the loudspeakers and mimed on stage. 'Mary' had learning disabilities, 'Jesus' had Down's syndrome. The story as told moved beyond scripture – for when Jesus appeared, he told Mary to fetch his brothers and sisters and tell them to love one another. 'Mary' fetched onto the stage a Cardinal from Italy, an Anglican bishop, a Roman Catholic archbishop from Canada, and a woman Methodist minister. We embraced and blessed the crowd together. Jesus with Down's syndrome brought representatives of his broken Body together.

I strongly recommend this book, with gratitude and renewed joy in all the riches God has showered upon us through loved ones who live with disability.

The Revd Professor Frances Young, OBE

---

* The L'Arche communities, founded by Jean Vanier, are places where people commit themselves to living in community with those who have learning disabilities; there are now around 130 communities all over the world. Faith and Light regularly gathers together those with learning disabilities living at home, with their families and friends for fellowship and mutual support; they too are world-wide. Both organizations have a Roman Catholic foundation but, where appropriate, have broken across boundaries to become ecumenical and multi-faith.

Preface

I would not have chosen to think about disability if left to myself. Disability has, however, impacted our family in a variety of ways and has really forced some thinking out of me. There is a rose in our garden that flowers with a brilliant white flower in the summer. I am sadly no gardener, but I did happen to plant this rose and one day I would like to learn more about making things grow in the hope that I might discover some of the secrets of consistently producing beautiful flowers and tasty vegetables. Many of the other things that I have planted seem to have got lost in the soil. In truth, I really have very little idea of what will grow throughout the seasons of the year, and what will not, and while my wife seems to have a better grasp of things, the garden really just happens around me. In the same way, I am constantly surprised at what takes root in my life and grows into something that I could never have anticipated. I certainly did not expect this subject to get hold of me as it has, taking root in my imagination and growing in my mind.

I am not disabled and I cannot pretend to know what it must be like to have a disability of any kind. What I hope to be able to do is to describe instead what it is like to be in close relationship with somebody who has a disability. The obvious fact is that none of us lives in isolation from others. It is therefore important to ask not simply what it is like to be disabled, but to ask what it is like to be disabled *in relationship to those who are not disabled*. A life, whether it is affected by disability or not, can only be studied when it intersects and interacts with other lives. When that happens, when two or more lives inhabit the same space or share the same experience either briefly or for decades, something else is created, something new is brought into being. This applies to colleagues, friends, neighbours and marriage partners. I cannot, as I have said, say anything authentic about what it is like to be disabled, but I can speak from a little more experience about this new thing that is created when one's life becomes interwoven with that of another who happens to be disabled.

It is a central understanding of Christian faith that God, in Jesus Christ, has quite deliberately chosen to interweave his life with ours. This, we believe, has created something new and I want to start by asking what new thing exactly has God created by acting in this way? I want then to go on pursuing the theme of creation because creation seems often to be regarded as something intended for the able-bodied, in which the disabled at best do not quite fit and at worst are considered to be a mistake. But I want to look at the stories of creation and 'the fall', and the promise of new creation, from the perspective of disability and to ask whether we should treat these major biblical themes differently as a result. Finally, I want to look at some universal implications for Christian discipleship that follow from an examination of these themes in creation. These last two chapters are considered in the context of attempting to understand what compassion is all about and how we can fulfil our vocation to live compassionate lives.

This is not in any way a definitive understanding of the Christian approach to these issues. Although not written about very extensively, there are still some much more scholarly books than mine written about these things. It is also important to say at the outset that I owe a great debt of thanks to a number of people whose wisdom and time have helped to develop these thoughts. I want to thank Melvyn Matthews for the encouragement to start writing in the first place, James and Alison Place for introducing us to Mantegna and his picture and Professor Frances Young for writing the Foreword. I want to acknowledge the collective wisdom and inspiration of the special needs team at New Wine Christian Conferences, Heather, Wendy, Caroline, Debbie-Jo and about twenty or thirty other very dedicated and wonderful colleagues. I want to thank the congregation at St Michael's, Bath, for showing us as a family so much care and compassion over the last ten years in very many practical ways. I am very grateful to the Corea family and to Helen who were prepared to tell me their own stories and allow me to reproduce them. A few people were kind enough to examine the manuscript before publication: Peter Lloyd Williams, Penny Faux and my wife Jackie. Their comments have been hugely helpful. It is, in fact, to Jackie and our children Tegan, Benedict and Holly that I am most grateful. They have seen even less of me than usual during the six months that this project has been in the pipeline but their encouragement has meant everything. Finally, any mistakes or muddles contained in these pages are, without any doubt, all my own doing.

1

So many questions

Listen to me, O coastlands,
pay attention, you peoples from far away!
The Lord called me from before I was born,
while I was in my mother's womb he named me.
He made my mouth like a sharp sword,
in the shadow of his hand he hid me;
he made me like a polished arrow,
in his quiver he hid me away.

Isaiah 49.1–2

Therefore, if anyone has been able to hold in the breadth of his mind, and to consider the glory and splendour of all those things created in him, he will be struck by their very beauty and transfixed by the magnificence of their brilliance or, as the prophet says, 'by the chosen arrow' (Isaiah 49.2). And he will receive from him the saving wound and will burn with blessed fire of his love.

Origen

I have yet to meet a person who is not moved, often to tears, by the birth of a child. My wife tells me it was a great help having me present at the birth of our own children, but I remember feeling helpless. When the hours of struggle finally gave way to the joy of a pink, startled baby the emotion was intense. So much relief, so much hope and joy and love. It was almost as if this event had never happened before in the whole history of the universe. After the birth of our second child, however, when I looked at him and saw his face, I was immediately concerned. Twice I asked the midwife if everything was as it should be and she reassured me that all was well. A little while later the paediatrician arrived and examined our son. He looked at his fingers, he felt his head and explored the soft areas below his newborn hair. He examined the gap between his big toe and the other toes. What he found led him to believe that our son, in all probability, had Down's syndrome. This diagnosis, he told us, would need to be confirmed by a blood test that would seek to identify an extra chromosome on the twenty-first gene. The blood test soon followed and the extra chromosome was indeed discovered. A microscopic, tiny additional chromosome that would change his life, and the life of our family, in every way. How could something that small have such a huge impact?

Questions immediately started darting through my brain. At first, they were not the philosophical questions but the practical questions. Would he walk? Would he speak? Would he live independently? What of sort of life lay ahead? Then we received from one of our son's godparents a picture by Andreas Mantegna, painted around 1465 and called *The Presentation at the Temple*.

I have studied the painting a great deal over the last thirteen years and continue to be drawn by its power to tell the story of what happened to the infant Jesus brought to the Temple in Jerusalem by Joseph and Mary.

Simeon (who we assume was an old man) had been given a promise by God that he would not die until he had seen the Lord's Christ. He was waiting for the consolation of Israel. It may well be that he had been waiting for the consolation of Israel for a very long time and, if this was the case, he must have wondered if he was not deluded. Possibly he even doubted himself. The initial moment of God's revelation had been marvellous and vivid but it had also been a long time ago and he could never have imagined that he would still be waiting all these years later for the promise to be fulfilled. Perhaps, in his darker moments, he sometimes wondered if he had missed it. Maybe he had been in the wrong place at the wrong time. Maybe he had committed some sin that had caused the Lord to change his mind.

And then one day the Holy Spirit guided him to the Temple and he saw what at first was an unexceptional family. There was nothing about the man, the woman or the child that made them stand out, but God spoke and Simeon knew that God's promise had been fulfilled. Where, however, was the consolation for which he had waited all these years? Where was the new Israel? Where was the restoration and renewal of the nation's life? Where was the rule of God? Simeon had waited a long time and had never seen any of these things. He had never seen the consolation of Israel. However, he sang a prophetic song that thanked God for keeping his promise. Then he spoke another prophetic word directly to Mary: 'This child is destined for the falling and the rising of many in Israel, and to be a sign that will be opposed so that the inner thoughts of many will be revealed – and a sword will pierce your own soul too' (Luke 2.34–35).

Mantegna's painting captures the moment, I believe, when the old man hands the baby Jesus back to his mother. It was not how he expected things to turn out. Joseph is in the middle of the picture, looking at Simeon, but is confined to the background. (We often believe ourselves to be at the centre of things when actually our role is to be a facilitator

3

and onlooker at the time and a witness later.) There is real intensity in the look shared between Simeon and Mary. Simeon has just spoken his ominous word and is handing Jesus back as if he is too hot to handle. Mary's right arm is holding her son tightly and protectively. She has pulled Jesus closely to herself so that their faces are touching. The atmosphere is very charged. Mantegna manages to let us see that both Mary and Simeon know at a deep level that God is at work.

I remember the words of the paediatrician, not because they were prophetic but because they too were heavy words to hear after he had handed back our son. Simeon had hoped for consolation and we had hoped for a 'perfect' child. However, the reason that our friend had sent us this painting was because it is believed that Mantegna has depicted the baby Jesus as a boy with Down's syndrome. I have tried to understand the artist better but it is quite difficult to penetrate Mantegna's motives for painting Jesus in this way. Some experts tell us that the slightly earlier sculptor, Donatello, influenced Mantegna in the way he painted faces in particular. Why, though, did he paint Jesus like this? At the time of painting, the artist was living and working in Mantua, which was not renowned in Italy as a great artistic centre. Patronage was confined to the Gonzaga court. Maybe a child with Down's syndrome had been born to a member of the court and Mantegna had been commissioned to paint Jesus in this way. We do not know.

The old man, Simeon, looked for consolation but received an epiphany moment. We so often expect our own faith to be about the provision of consolation, the righting of wrongs and the immediate defeat of evil, but if we are not careful and attentive to the movement of God's Holy Spirit we can become fixated by the things that God has not promised us and, in fact, miss the opportunity to hear or speak a prophetic word and encounter the living, life-changing God whose purpose is vastly beyond our imagination and whose desire and passion is for us to be fully alive and completely human.

Completely human. What does that mean? Everybody struggles to find their identity and the purpose for their life. Rick Warren's excellent book, *The Purpose Driven Life*, has sold in millions because it seeks to help people find answers for these deep questions of meaning and purpose. When we think of someone with a disability it is so easy to think first about the things they cannot do and focus on their limitations. My wife has to use a wheelchair for distances further than about a hundred metres, and even today, if I am pushing her, people we meet will still ask *me* how she is rather than speak to *her*! Many people seem to assume that it is not really appropriate for a disabled person to think about what it is that makes them human since only those with normal bodies and fully functional minds can aspire to being human.

What God has chosen

If this is the attitude of a great many people today, what is the attitude of God towards the disabled? Mantegna's painting has become an incredibly provocative piece of art for me and introduced me to a number of questions. My first reaction to it thirteen years ago was to find it cute: how lovely, I thought, Jesus has a special place for babies with Down's syndrome. But the problem is that babies with Down's syndrome grow into teenagers just like everybody else. They do not grow out of Down's syndrome. And then the penny dropped. Mantegna is suggesting that Jesus *could have chosen* to be born with Down's syndrome without that affecting the purpose of the incarnation. Can he possibly be right? Could the incarnate Son of God have fulfilled his divine destiny if he had been born with a learning disability? This is the first big question I want to ask.

I gradually began to realize that this question affected the whole way we understand how creation works. We operate with a mindset that is predominantly one of cause and effect. In order to achieve a particular result, we think to ourselves, we need to initiate a particular cause. In order to get to a particular place, we need a particular set of pre-defined circumstances that will set this journey in motion. This cause-and-effect understanding of the world is in turn based upon Newtonian physics which is heavily deterministic. That is to say that by measuring everything, it should be theoretically possible for the future to be determined or predicted. Scientists in the last hundred years, however, have realized that all is not so simple. Quantum physics and chaos theory have introduced the notion of unpredictability in particular. Creation is more complicated than we previously thought. What a surprise!

But what has all this to do with disability and the purpose of the incarnation? When we address the question of why God became human, our first reflex seems to be to want to talk about the things that Jesus came to *achieve*. Inevitably, therefore, we move to explanations and doctrines; we use legal terminology and phrases such as substitutionary atonement, which attempt to state plainly and clearly that if God were to achieve the desired effect of salvation and redemption, a number of specific criteria would first have to be met. If Jesus' purpose is defined primarily in terms of a task that he had to achieve then it is difficult to see how he could have been successful had he been born with a learning disability, and Mantegna would be leading us in the wrong direction. However, maybe the superseding of Newtonian cause-and-effect thinking can help us to understand creation differently and can open us up to the possibility of recognizing a creator who is passionate about his creation and who, quite literally, throws himself recklessly into it in the incarnation. He does this not simply because he wants to effect a particular result, but because he cannot bear to be apart from it, because he is intrinsically bound up with its destiny, because it is his very nature to continually pour himself out. If this whirlwind of passion has as its primary desire the intention of drawing all creation and all creatures back to the source of all life, is it not possible to see a more complex, mystical process at work that we need not so much to be explained as to be caught up in? And if this is the case, if God's desire is to elicit from us reciprocal love and fierce devotion, maybe it is also important for him to be incarnate in a way that draws from us a similarly selfless love that, in the first instance at least, offers no guarantee of material reward. If God is calling us to love him for himself, rather than with the intention of our obtaining something, what better way to come among us than as a person with learning impairments who, in worldly terms, can offer little or any return on the emotional investment we are making. If this is right, Mantegna may be on to something.

Certainly, until around the seventeenth century, this mystical approach to faith would have found many more exponents and practitioners than is the case today. Writers like Origen in the third century, Bernard of Clairvaux in the

7

twelfth, Teresa of Avila and John of the Cross in the sixteenth century all sought to give emphasis to the wildly passionate character of God. One of Bernard of Clairvaux's best-known works is his famous *On the Love of God*. Here he talks about the four stages, or degrees, of love. He writes:

> You ask me, 'Why should God be loved?' I answer: the reason for loving God is God himself. And why should God be loved for his own sake? Simply because no one could be more justly loved than God, no one deserves our love more. Some may question if God deserves our love or if they might have something to gain by loving him. The answer to both questions is yes, but I find no other worthy reason for loving him except himself.

As Bernard points out, many people do indeed ask if God deserves our love and one reason for this question is the presence of disability (as well as other forms of suffering) in the world. What is therefore so challenging about Mantegna's painting is the way it turns this question on its head. Instead of disability being the cause of questioning God's love, it is seen as the vehicle for drawing people to it. We must not then go down the romantic, but offensive, way of thinking that would have us believe that suffering is beautiful if it brings us closer to God. Suffering is never beautiful. The trauma surrounding disability is intense. God, I believe, hates the pain that it causes and the Bible is clear that pain (though not disability) has no place in the new heaven and the new earth that are to come. And this is why we need to remember those people who have written on the mystical way throughout the history of the Church. We do not know what to do with disability because we have really lost sight of what it is to be human, to be created and to be made in the image of God. Melvyn Matthews writes:

We have found ourselves in a position where theologically we have very few resources to rescue us from fundamentalist understandings of the fallenness of humanity, while philosophically we have given ourselves little alternative to a thoroughly activist view of the springs of human life.[1]

So what has Jesus come to do? In Philippians 2 it says that Jesus gave everything up. This means he had nothing to offer but himself. On the night before he died, when he took bread and wine and said this is my body and this is my blood, this is what I am giving you, it was because he had nothing else left to give them. Everything else had been given up. It has been said that generosity is when somebody with plenty gives something to somebody who has nothing and gives out of his or her power, wealth or knowledge. Communion, on the other hand, is when you do not give things, you give yourself. It is about trust and love. Most of us are better at giving things than we are at trusting ourselves to others. Jesus, however, gave himself. Many people with learning disabilities will never be able to be generous in the way of the world but they can and often do lead the way when it comes to giving themselves. Henri Nouwen makes the point that in terms of being able to offer a material return on the investment made in them, handicapped people have little to offer. And yet they do offer us such treasure. They give themselves. By not paying us for what they do, they call us to the inner freedom found in selflessness, generosity and true care.

Delighting in humanity

Here is my second big question: if we do not have a good understanding of what it means to be human, how much can we *value* being human? I said before that God wants us to be completely human, but I am not sure how many people really believe that to be true. Neither am I sure how many people really want God to make us fully human. I meet many people who, it would appear, want to escape being human. I meet people who intensely dislike their bodies, people who are sadly fearful of interacting with other people. I come across others who have been so starved of love and affirmation, and are sometimes so full of anger, that relationships are impossible. Many of these people are earning big salaries. I encounter those who seem almost afraid of interacting with their environments: earphones go in as soon as they leave their front door; all eye contact is avoided; expensive car windows are always rolled up, the air con is at full blast and the CD changer makes sure that the sounds of the world around are firmly excluded. Behaviour like this is indicative of an attitude that denies a traditional understanding of how we become more complete human beings, namely by accepting our bodies, by living in constructive relationships with others and by connecting to our physical environments. (This is to say nothing of the way our fractured relationship with the earth itself affects our understanding of what it is to be human, a theme I want to return to.)

So, I am not sure if we have much desire to accept our humanity today. How many of us are comfortable with people different from ourselves? How many of us like our bodies? How many of us, either out of pride or from fear of litigation, can admit our failures? How many of us are tempted to live in a fantasy environment instead of our real environment? Virtual reality is available virtually all of the time. In truth, many people explore Christianity hoping that it will become a way of escaping from being human, not because they want to become more fully the person God created them to be. Sadly, there are those in the Church who teach a form a Gnosticism that encourages such a search by suggesting the material fabric of the world is totally corrupt, including our own bodies, and that the point of Christian spirituality is to escape into a type of spiritual otherness that is free from the taint of all material things.

Mantegna's painting says to me that God *wanted* to become human so badly that he would go to the extent of accepting disability in order to become human. In fact, Jesus could reasonably have described any form of becoming human as accepting a disability, because 'though he was in the form of God, [he] did not regard equality with God as something to be exploited, but emptied himself, taking the form of a slave' (Philippians 2.6–7). Mantegna's painting speaks to me of a God who effectively says, 'Learning disabled, physically disabled, able bodied, they are all the same to me, it doesn't matter who I choose to be like, I just want to be human!' This is hard for us to believe when people all around us are screaming to shed their humanity. But there is no reluctance in the incarnation. There is no sense of last resort. There was clearly celebration in the heavenly realms on the night that Jesus was born and it spilled over into the whole Judaean countryside. God was seriously excited about becoming human and we would do well to be excited about being human too. We would do well to be more aware of the subtle pulls and influences in our own society, and in our churches, that whisper to us the lie that our humanity is completely bad and beyond redemption and therefore should be jettisoned. Remember the famous words of Irenaeus, 'The glory of God is man fully alive.'

The God who needs an invitation

I have another copy of a Madonna and Child painting at home by the contemporary artist Paul Hobbs. It is a beautiful picture based on an Ethiopian woman carrying her baby on her hip. Its original context was that of famine and its message, I believe, is that God is present even in such awful situations as mass starvation in sub-Saharan Africa. In the last forty years a new understanding of the incarnation has resulted in many artists painting images of Christ as a black African or as an Asian or a South American. They are powerful representations of the truth that while Jesus was undeniably Jewish, the purpose of his coming, and the scope of the salvation he offers, is for people of every race and ethnicity. Artists painting Jesus in these ways want to say to others of their own race or culture, 'Jesus is like you and for you.' But this raises a third question for me: does the same principle apply to portrayals of Jesus as disabled? We can say to the disabled community, along with artists from Africa, Asia or South America, that, of course, Jesus' purpose is to include you too, but is Mantegna placing the emphasis in a different place with his painting of the Presentation of Christ at the Temple?

There are stories in the Gospels of Jesus reaching out to Gentiles: the woman at the well who had been married many times, the Canaanite woman who memorably replied to Jesus that even the dogs could eat the crumbs that fall from the master's table, the centurion with a sick servant who felt unworthy to have Jesus come to his house. Jesus welcomed such 'outsiders' and even marvelled at their faith. But when it came to the disabled, his desire was to heal. It seems as if Jesus could accept people from different ethnic backgrounds just as they were but did not accept the disabled in the same way. There were no disabled people in Jesus' retinue. So what is going on?

It is clear from both the Gospels and from the way artists from different cultures have interpreted Jesus that God wants to reach out to people of every culture and draw them into the orbit of his Kingdom. The message is that all those who may have thought themselves to be beyond the reach of God need no longer consider themselves to be outsiders but are as welcome as anybody else to the wedding feast of the Lamb. Come to Jesus and freely enter. The emphasis is on adoption of the outsiders with the purpose of making them insiders. With Mantegna, however, there is a different emphasis. Jesus is seen not as the giver of invitations to the heavenly party but as the outsider who himself needs to receive a welcome.

This is a sentiment picked up by the German theologian Jürgen Moltmann who said that Jesus was the man crucified not between two candles on an altar but crucified as an outsider, between two criminals, in the place of the skull. This is an important statement that reflects how many people with disabilities and their families and carers feel that they too are often regarded as outsiders. Sometimes this is because our society is poor at inclusion and sometimes this is simply because a disability means that fewer options are open. In our own family, for example, a straightforward exercise like walking the dog is an activity that only three of the five of us can participate in. This is nobody's fault, but it is important, as a Christian, to know that God expresses his solidarity with this situation.

In his book *The Crucified God*, Jürgen Moltmann quotes from Dietrich Bonhoeffer's letters from prison. Bonhoeffer writes:

13

God lets himself be pushed out of the world on to the cross. He is weak and powerless in the world, and that is precisely the way, the only way, in which he is with us and helps us. Matthew 8.17 makes it quite clear that Christ helps us, not by virtue of his omnipotence, but by virtue of his weakness and suffering . . . Only the suffering God can help . . . That is a reversal of what the religious man expects from God. Man is summoned to share in God's sufferings at the hands of a godless world.[2]

God's identification with the poor and marginalized, his solidarity with those on the edge of society, is such that God needs us to invite him back again into the mainstream of everyday life. Of course, some with disabilities will react strongly against the suggestion that they should see themselves as marginalized or peripheral, but exclusion is the experience of many whether or not they have the strength of character to challenge the status quo. Moltmann and Bonhoeffer are both provoking us to think of God in an uncomfortable way. They are asking us to contemplate a God who gives everything up in order to reveal love. The powerlessness of God, as they describe it, is deeply disturbing. Rather than resolving the chaos of life, everything seems to get worse. But there are other aspects of God's work that remain hidden at the moment of his death, just as they were at the moment of his birth. The Bible does not portray the dying Jesus as a helpless victim but as a willing sacrifice. Jesus suffers as a result of the choices he makes, not because he finally runs out of luck in his conflict with the authorities. Jesus chooses to go to Jerusalem knowing he will be crucified; he was not simply in the wrong place at the wrong time.

Moltmann repeatedly stresses this identification of Jesus with the marginalized and excluded:

The dominant church has from earliest times so formu-
lated . . . the cross that believers are made aware only of the
pains caused to Christ by their individual sins and their
private immorality. But the poor no doubt recognise all
their suffering in the crucified Christ: what they suffered
from society and what they suffered from their fate.[3]

The Jesus whom Moltmann describes is easy to ignore, to
push to the periphery or to place in a care home. He is easy
to patronize and easy to think of as an object of pity. But
just as the world attempts to treat Jesus in this way, having
managed to entomb him safely in a residential care establishment, we come back the following morning to find that
the doors of the home have been completely blown off and
the inmates all gone. Somehow, in the choice that the Son
of God makes to identify with the least of the least, God does
far more than simply say, 'There there, I know how it feels.'
In choosing to become the least of all, Jesus subverts the world,
fulfils his divine destiny and sets free all those captives who
agree to join him in the Great Breakout. But the world had
to be subverted first. The Son of God had to come as one
needing to receive the heavenly invitation to new life on behalf
of a world that for so long had been unable even to get dressed
for the heavenly party.

My children sometimes play hide and seek. One of them
counts to fifty while the others hide. When the counting is
over, and before starting to look for the others, the 'seeker'
shouts out, 'Coming, ready or not!' I believe that this is what
God shouts out to his world, 'Coming, ready or not!' The
Son of God's arrival in the world, while anticipated, was still
a surprise and a shock. Look at Zechariah, the father of John
the Baptist, look at Mary, remember the shepherds. It is as
if God was saying to them, 'Here I come, ready or not!' The

lack of space at the inn at Bethlehem is wonderfully symbolic of a world not being ready.

Remember also the Jesus who called the unsuspecting fishermen to follow him, or the funeral at Nain that Jesus suddenly interrupted. Think of the disillusioned Nathaniel who believed that nothing good could come out of Nazareth before he met Jesus. Recall those who encountered Jesus after the resurrection outside the tomb, by the lakeside, or on the way to Emmaus. To each person, and to us, Jesus says, in effect, 'Coming, ready or not!'

I wonder if the world can ever be ready for Mantegna's Jesus? I wonder if the artist asks too much of us? Ultimately, the searing compassion of God becomes the foundation for the coming Kingdom and a crucial element in all the works and teaching of Jesus. I want to continue looking in particular at the role that disability plays in our practice of compassion and our subsequent experience of the power of God's coming Kingdom. I am not sure that Mary and Joseph were ready for Mantegna's Jesus. Sometimes I feel like Mary. I find myself recoiling from the less comfortable aspects of Jesus' ministry and hoping that my own relationship with Jesus will lead me only beside still waters. I certainly find myself watching as Joseph seems to be watching; trying to get as close to the action as possible but somehow feeling slightly peripheral all the same. But maybe watching God at work would be a habit we could all usefully cultivate as part of our spiritual discipline. Meanwhile, in Mantegna's painting at least, this little *disabled* child is at the centre of the action. A prophetic word has been uttered about him and on him are the hopes of the world.

2

Is God really disabled?

————•◦•————

All feelings of disappointment with God trace back to a
breakdown in that relationship. Thus, I determined to look
for the answer to a question I had never before considered:
'What does it feel like to be God?'[4]

Philip Yancey

What indeed is it like to be God? Awesome? Invincible?
Omnipotent? In her novel *Mr Golightly's Holiday*, Sally
Vickers asks this question. Mr Golightly arrives in the quiet
Devon village of Great Calne for some time to relax and
to reacquaint himself with the world that he has created
because, unbeknown to the assorted, dysfunctional inhabit-
ants of the village, Mr Golightly is actually God. His stay in
Great Calne turns out to be anything but an uneventful time
as it coincides with the unravelling of many of the fragile
lives of the people who live there, and leads the central character to reflect on his own part in the mess of the world. It
is on Mr Golightly's mind that he might update the Bible in
the form of a soap opera so as to better connect with a more
popular audience. With so much to occupy his thoughts, he
often walks up onto the moor to think about things.

A little way off stood a group of Dartmoor ponies, two the
almost-black brown of their breed and one, larger, hardly a

17

pony at all, a ghostly white. Their manes lifted in the breeze as, begging no favours and enjoining no compunction, they patiently cropped the perpetually renewing vegetable carpet of the Moor.

Mr Golightly gazed for a long while on the scene before him. His was an imagination which, in its time, had fashioned many and diverse things. The imagination is a creator of worlds – and from his had issued gods and kingdoms, peoples and purposes, stables and citadels, deserts and mountain tops, the defeat of principalities, the frail victory of hope. Before him now, the sun was perfecting its own creation, sprinkling the vegetation with a shifting silver sheen. Out of the cool earth, through the sun's unflagging warmth, sprang herbs and grasses and trees. And deep within the earth's fiery centre its power formed the ores of precious metals, silver and gold – emblems of human nobility. But where was that nobility realised on earth?

Not, to be sure, among the population of Great Calne. It seemed that such virtues had faded from the world, leaving behind only a rusty stain. Perhaps the failure lay in him? Maybe his creative powers, on which so much of his identity had been based, had all been a sham, and the world which had once seemed so various, so beautiful, so new was nothing more than a darkling plain, swept with confused alarms of struggle and flight . . .

He had come away for a rest, a holiday, yet he found he was tired: tired of trying to dodge people who wanted something incalculable from him, tired of trying to master the tricks of a world which seemed to have shot ahead of him, tired of his efforts to weave the lives of those he had created into his idea for a soap opera. Tired, in short, of the memorials of his own inadequate vocation. It was a footling, foolhardy, crackbrained scheme – he'd do best to abandon it, return to his former privacy and allow the slow seepage of his fame to continue unarrested. Who would miss him, after all?[5]

As I said in the previous chapter, the idea of God allowing himself to be marginalized in the world he has created is not without theological precedent. The idea of God being sidelined is very much a part of the theology of Jürgen Moltmann. Sally Vickers' novel allows us to speculate not so much about the theological correctness of such a proposition but to ask the rather more personal question of how God feels about this. It also introduces the idea of just how far God is prepared to go in order to connect with the world he loves. Would he go as far as becoming disabled?

For many people the first problem to get over when asking the question 'Is God disabled?' is the (usually subliminal) presupposition that people with disabilities are in some way less human, incomplete, or generally 'not as good' as those without disabilities. If God were to become human, so the argument runs, he would need to be the best possible human imaginable, the finest specimen conceivable. The idea therefore that the incarnate God might be disabled is a non-starter. An incomplete God, or a lesser God, is not only unappealing, it appears a contradiction in terms. Some people will protest vigorously that they have no such prejudices, that they do not at all consider people with disabilities 'lesser', but I would contend that it is never wise to claim freedom from prejudice.

When it was announced that Paul McCartney and Heather Mills McCartney had agreed to separate, their marriage was discussed on Radio Four. I was amazed how, during this discussion, I counted over a dozen jokes made about the fact that Heather Mills McCartney has a prosthetic leg. Would such jokes have been made in this manner had she been a member of an ethnic or religious minority group? When I lead seminars on incorporating people with learning disabilities into the life of the Church, one question I am always asked is how can we stop people with learning disabilities shouting out loudly and disturbing our services? I usually reply that it's their service too and ask why it is such a problem. We are currently in the process of introducing disabled access into our church building and it has taken five years to convince enough people (but not everybody) that it is unacceptable to ask wheelchair users to enter via a separate entrance round the back, through the toilets and past the cleaning cupboard. The fact that the few wheelchair users who visit us say that they really don't mind this humiliation is to miss the point – which is that by doing this the stereotype of the disabled person as a lesser person is perpetuated.

Another attitude that gets in the way of us even beginning to address the question of the disability of God is the overly romantic notion of heroic suffering and virtuous patience that we link to the disabled. This attitude perpetuates the notion that the ideal disabled person is one who quietly goes about their business in their own limited world, nobly putting up with the lot that fate has dealt them as an example to the rest of us that we should be more thankful for our own blessings. Such attitudes continue to deny people with disabilities the opportunities to develop as people, as well as denying the rest of us the benefit of their many talents. Of course there are inspirational stories about people overcoming huge disabilities, but what most people are looking for are not medals but the opportunities to live an ordinary life.

Again, people with learning difficulties are often treated as objects for charity. This attitude, while nearly always well intentioned, reduces people to being merely objects. It certainly does not leave much room for people with learning disabilities to make a contribution in their own right, or to be empowered to have some say in their own futures. I have come across the other side of this coin in church life as well. I have heard it said that it is important for people with learning impairments to be able to understand, for example, all the words of the worship songs they sing in church. While this might seem sensible, it frequently (though not always) results in the use of worship songs of such banal quality as to be ridiculous. Teenagers with Down's syndrome, for example, enjoy the sort of modern worship songs, often in a rock idiom, that most other teenage Christians want to hear. I can remember a girl called Rosie, who had severe learning difficulties. Her favourite worship song was 'My Jesus My Saviour'. She didn't understand all the words but she knew that Jesus was hers and that he was her saviour, and she was an inspirational worshipper who enabled others to come into the presence of God. It is not good enough for teenagers to be singing the songs of a five-year-old simply because they have a learning disability.

These are some of the attitudes that, whether or not we admit to holding them ourselves, are out there in the Church and in the world. Until we are able to get some of these attitudes into the light we will not have the necessary openness of mind to begin to talk about our God as being the Disabled God.

We have already looked at the great hymn quoted by St Paul in Philippians 2, but I want to turn to it again in order to comprehend fully the drama of what is being claimed here:

> Let the same mind be in you that was in Christ Jesus, who,
> though he was in the form of God, did not regard equality
> with God as something to be exploited, but emptied himself,
> taking the form of a slave, being born in human likeness.
> (Philippians 2.5–7)

Jesus, the Son of God, made himself nothing. The Greek words convey the sense of this with more stark power. The Greek says that Jesus stripped himself, he emptied himself, he became a slave. The meaning is that Jesus could get no lower. He was low to the point of embarrassment. To get a sense of just how extreme God's behaviour is in the incarnation, picture a dramatic scene from the early life of Francis of Assisi. Francis and his father had a seriously dysfunctional relationship. Francis had, in fact, stolen quite a lot of his father's money to fund his obsessional quest to rebuild the church of San Damiano. Being completely furious and at the end of his tether, his father hauled Francis off to face the local bishop whom he hoped would restore some filial respect as well as the property that had been stolen. In response to the charges, and against the beautiful medieval backdrop of Assisi in April 1206, Francis simply removed all his clothes and stood naked before the court. He returned his clothes to his father and declared that his father no longer had any power over him. There was no going back. It was a dramatic, powerful and, it must be said, eccentric gesture. In England in 2006, eight hundred years later, he would have been arrested. But in a way he was simply copying Jesus. He had placed himself utterly in the hands of the world, of other people and of God. He had no choice but to leave Assisi for Gubbio where he had some friends. Those who passed him on the road recalled that he sang out loudly and in French as if he was mad. It was as if the song he was singing was truly foreign to the world of his day.

To be naked, vulnerable and in the hands of others was the experience of Jesus and is, often quite literally, the experience of many with disabilities. When we read Philippians 2 we need to be reawakened to the starkness of what is happening to God and sensitive to the emotional response that is then naturally provoked within us. We may feel moved. We may feel inspired. We may be awestruck. But are we embarrassed? God is stripping in front of the world! God is going naked! Shouldn't we be just a little bit shocked? I can remember being shocked as a teenager when I first saw images of Simon Weston, the former soldier, who was terribly burned during the Falklands war. I was shocked this year on visiting India (despite previous trips) to see so many people with disabilities begging around traffic lights and having no option but to ignore their pleas and hope the lights would go green quickly. I think St Paul is encouraging a similar response when we consider Jesus. I have often considered the image from Revelation of Jesus standing at the door and knocking, but in Delhi it struck me that he was also standing at my car window and knocking and I was reminded that what I do for the least of people I also do for him. Jesus is, St Paul says to me, one who, like many disabled people, causes a mixed reaction of shock and embarrassment. The polarity of embarrassment and beauty, something which makes us draw back and something which irresistibly attracts, is a polarity which is displayed in the person of Jesus and is a useful polarity to hold on to if we are to get inside a theology of disability.

I do not want to conclude from all this that Jesus gives us a mandate to be an embarrassment to the Kingdom of God.

What I mean is that because of the way Jesus is incarnate in the world, and because of the way in which he was rejected through the cross, Jesus stirs up a similar reaction to that which many disabled people find they also provoke from a staring world. This is the starting place, the first point of commonality shared by Jesus and the disabled community. Neither Jesus nor those with disabilities deliberately embark on a mission to shock, but, as the Prologue to John's Gospel reminds us, Jesus came to his own and his own did not receive him. The same can still be true today for people with disabilities. Attitudes and issues of access create barriers and handicaps that prevent people being 'received' by their own. Struggle for access to education, welfare provision and other support, such as respite care, is still the common experience of many parents with disabled children. Such parents have no desire to act in militant ways but their experience does provide a point of contact with Jesus who was also not received.

The question, however, still needs to be addressed: in what way, if any, is the incarnate God disabled? After all, Jesus was young, male and Jewish. He appeared to be in rude health throughout his life. He cured disability, he didn't have one. The incarnation itself represents such a major abandonment of power and ability that it could legitimately be described as an experience akin to disablement. It is, however, at the crucifixion and resurrection of Jesus that, in a physical way, and in comparison to other human beings, the incarnate God could be said to be genuinely disabled. Theologian Amanda Shao Tan points out:

> It was on the cross that Jesus experienced the ultimate disability. Pinned to the cross, he knew how it felt to be physically incapacitated. The pains and struggles which he faced were similar to the ones endured by those with disabilities.

Since disability and sickness were considered as preliminary forms of death, Jesus went through an analogous death experience. On the cross, he was regarded as a sinner, one who was forsaken by God – an image regularly applied to the disabled.[6]

It has also been pointed out that the prophecy of Isaiah 53, stating that the suffering servant would be 'as one from whom others hide their faces', is a prophecy fulfilled at the crucifixion of Jesus and could be taken as meaning that the punishment received by Jesus left him both disabled and disfigured. So Jesus did understand physical limitations. But what about the resurrection? Is the risen Jesus still disabled or was disability removed on Easter morning? The remarkable answer, of course, is that the risen Jesus continues to bear the wounds of suffering. In fact these wounds became the means for at least one disciple of ascertaining his identity. 'Put your finger into my wounds,' said Jesus. What were the nature of the wounds that remained?

As an aside, I have sometimes wondered if the scars of Jesus were only marks on his skin, or were they deeper, leaving for ever the flesh and sinews (though not the bone) under his skin also eternally damaged and scarred? Although this is an odd, and ultimately speculative piece of curiosity, I find the possibility that Jesus may consequently have been limping along the road to Emmaus stimulates a potentially powerful image. After all, anyone with ruptured ankles or feet would undoubtedly have had difficulty walking and, if the wounds of Jesus remain for a purpose, surely that purpose goes beyond being a mere display, a mark of identification, or a reminder of Calvary. The sin of the world has for ever impacted the very being of the Son of God. In the same way that Jacob's wrestling with the angel at the Jabbok river left him permanently limping, the Son of God's conflict with evil does not leave him unscathed. All this will, of course, have to remain speculation. But there is no doubting that the risen Jesus mysteriously retains his impairment to hands and feet and side. This matters, of course, because Jesus was not only a man with disability, he was also God, and through the experience of the cross became, and is for ever, the Disabled God. This consequently raises questions about the way we use some of our inherited Christian symbolism to express what we believe – particularly the symbolism of the body.

Together, Christians are the Body of Christ. But what sort of body do we imagine ourselves to be? Most of us experience life as able-bodied people and we therefore take that to be normative. To be fair, this would seem to be the way St Paul also imagined things when writing Romans, 1 Corinthians and Ephesians. But look at the encounter that the risen Jesus had with the disciples in a locked room as reported in John 20. It was evening time; the room was probably not well lit. The atmosphere was tense and the discussion was probably going round in circles: where was the body of Jesus? The door was locked and the inmates were worried that any knock on it might be the Jewish authorities arriving to arrest them. Suddenly, Jesus miraculously appeared. 'Peace be with you', he said. Then he showed them his hands and side. The whole room, John reports, gave a collective sigh of relief, but Jesus had not appeared simply to cheer them up. He wanted to restate the same calling he had given them three years earlier when they were still catching fish, collecting taxes and plotting revolution. I am sending you out, he told them, just as the Father himself sent me out. The idea of sending them out seemed faintly ridiculous. They were terrified about leaving the room! I am reminded at this point of the prayer of Mother Teresa of Calcutta. He has no hands or feet now but ours, she said. The followers of Jesus are sent out to be the Body of Christ, his hands and his feet. The juxtaposition of this commission with the fresh revelation of his own wounded hands and feet makes a significant statement. You are to be a body after the fashion of my crucified body, my now disabled body, Jesus is saying, not after the fashion of my previous, pre-crucifixion body.

In the light of this, when we think about our understanding of ourselves as the Body of Christ, maybe we should consider having in our minds the image of a disabled body as being an appropriate and normative image for the Church rather than an able-bodied image. Such an understanding is not only for the benefit of the disabled community, it is not a piece of politically correct theology, but is a means for those of us who are able bodied to be more open to spiritual renewal and mission.

The Church is not simply a group of people, even a group of Christian people, coming together because they think that to do so is a good idea. Karl Barth makes this clear:

> The Christian congregation arises and exists neither by nature nor by historical human decision, but as a divine *convocatio*. Those called together by the work of the Holy Spirit assemble at the summons of their King. Where the Church coincides with the natural living community, with, for example, that of the nation, the danger of a misunderstanding always threatens.[7]

The Church, the Body of Christ, is brought into being by the Holy Spirit who calls men and women to the ongoing ministry of Jesus Christ, to the work of being his hands and feet in the world. The Body of Christ cannot exist apart from the Holy Spirit, the Church cannot uphold itself, and therefore, as Barth goes on to say, cannot be governed either monarchically or democratically, but functions only under the direct rule of Christ through Word and Spirit. There are a number of implications here.

First, this means that a real possibility exists for the Church to be set free from what can so easily develop into a tyranny of trying to compete with the world on its own terms. The world does not need a Church that runs like a multinational company but a Church that offers grace by treating the unloved with dignity and by offering the powerful the opportunity to serve. This is not to say that the Church should be poorly administered or shabby in its presentation of the good news but that when we remember that the Body of Christ is a disabled body we can recover the perspective that compassion, not competition, is at the heart of the Kingdom of God, that our primary calling is to the process of living with integrity while letting God worry about results. This in turn should also free us from coveting what is happening in other churches or in the lives of other Christians. It should enable us to focus our best attention on God's agenda for the local church and to pray for local renewal of the Church without worrying about how we may be doing in comparison with others.

Second, it is important to remember that symbols have the power to shape the present and direct the future, and the symbol of the Disabled Body of Christ is a symbol that can potentially create corporate wholeness. We believe as Christians that our own wholeness in Christ, what is sometimes described with the beautiful Jewish word 'shalom', cannot be achieved as individuals. Wholeness is corporate or it is nothing. The suffering of our sisters and brothers in

Christ directly impacts on our own wholeness and the rebellion of the world against God is a disease that we are all caught up in. Corporate wholeness is to do with a widespread recognition that the problems of minority groups, in reality, affect us all. Nancy Eiesland, a North American writer on theology and disability as well as being a disabled person herself, writes:

> The perception that disability is a private, physical and emotional tragedy to be managed by psychological adjustment, rather than a stigmatised social condition to be redressed through attitudinal changes and social commitment to equality of opportunity for people with disabilities, is persistent.[8]

Eiesland is saying that disability affects us all. If we are harbouring attitudes or perpetuating practices that prevent disabled people from living ordinary, mainstream lives, then our own journey into wholeness will founder. Conversely, when the Body of Christ can start to exhibit corporate wholeness, through the rejection of discrimination, it starts to model and offer a genuinely counter-cultural alternative to all that is destructive and addictive in society.

This leads on to a third implication of our understanding the Body of Christ as a disabled body, namely that incompleteness is part of all human people. A young disabled woman called Stephanie once asked me why God had made her the way she was. I stumbled for an appropriate response but could not think of what to say. It was only later, as I was replaying the moment over in my mind, that it struck me that her question is one we should all be asking for ourselves. Her incompleteness was visible, mine was not. Henri Nouwen pointed out that during his time spent living with people with learning disabilities he learned that his own disabilities were of the heart, an inability to live out the gospel with simplicity and an inability to love unconditionally. Now, to some this will seem to belittle the real problems that people with physical disabilities have to cope with day by day. It would indeed be unhelpful to say to a person in a wheelchair, 'I know just how you must be feeling, I'm having a problem myself today with unconditional love'. However, what is helpful is when the barriers between the able-bodied and disabled communities come down sufficiently to enable a dialogue to take place that leads to greater understanding of just how incomplete all of us are as human beings. The important question that follows is: where will this discussion lead us? The response that the twenty-first century encourages us to make is to move quickly into activism, into the attempt to improve ourselves, or at least to do enough good things to obscure our incompleteness. The Church has all too often bought into this approach by a subtle emphasis on *agape* love, the doing of unconditional acts of kindness, that, when not securely linked to *eros* love, leads to burnout and disillusionment. Our response to incompleteness has been to place heavy emphasis on acts of commitment, human will-power and the importance of choice. These attitudes are the product of existentialist philosophies that place human freedom of action at the heart of the search for human identity. But the symbol of the Disabled Body of Christ draws us away from seeing human freedom and choice as being of primary importance, towards the idea that being listened to, understood and loved provides a more secure basis for human maturity. The image of the Disabled Body of Christ is one that helps us remember that the way of Jesus is the way of radical openness to God and to the world, or, put another way, fierce attentiveness to God and the world.

It is the insight of the contemplative tradition, stretching right back to the Desert Fathers, that none of us can find our true selves in isolation from others or from God. In fact there is no such thing as the self apart from relationship with the other. It is the loss of this insight that has undermined much of the Church's evangelistic endeavours over the last two hundred years in the face of the Enlightenment obsession with, and core belief in, the supremacy of the individual. The purpose of spirituality, including much Christian spirituality, has become horribly person-centred. It has become predominantly concerned with something that will help me to have a better life. The contemplative tradition, on the other hand, with its emphasis on radical openness to the other and the sheer compelling beauty of God, maintains that we are all incomplete works in progress. God is at work turning us inside out both for his glory and for our growth into maturity. To embrace the symbol of the Disabled Body of Christ is not to violate the glory of the risen and ascended Christ, neither is it to humiliate the Church, rather it is to embrace a symbol that facilitates participation in the life of God.

Participation in the life of God can only become a possibility when we reject a modernist way of viewing the self and recognize that there are other ways of realizing our identity and security that do not depend on us being able to earn more, buy more, consume more, learn more, or generally do more than my neighbour. The Disabled Christ is an icon that gives us access into an understanding that God is a source of life for all human beings, not simply a source of dogma used by some human beings to deny life to others. Such an icon dissolves the notion that it is the smartest and fittest who are most blessed by God. The Disabled Christ takes very seriously the presence of evil in the world. It is the powers and principalities of the world that play upon the fears and insecurities of human people. It is these fears and insecurities that opened the way for disability to be inflicted upon the Son of God at Calvary because they gave sin a foothold. The cross of Jesus Christ was not simply a piece of virtuous suffering but an act that supremely undermines the world's power structures, motivations and behaviour. It was not simply a piece of divine charitable action, but also a re-conciling moment within the person of God himself. And so another word from North American theologian Nancy Eiesland:

> As long as disability is addressed in terms of the themes of sin-disability conflation, virtuous suffering, or charitable action it will be seen primarily as a fate to be avoided, a tragedy to be explained or a cause to be championed rather than an ordinary life to be lived.[9]

3

Beauty, blessing and boundaries

—•◦•—

The order, arrangement, beauty, change and movement of the visible world declare that it could only have been the work of God, who is indescribably and invisibly great and indescribably and invisibly beautiful.[10]

St Augustine

Beauty

A little while ago we went to visit an exhibition of a friend's ceramics. It was a wonderful display of her final year's coursework and we were very excited because she had justifiably been awarded a first-class degree. As well as our friend's work, the exhibition included all sorts of pieces from other students, some of whom had already been 'talent spotted' by commercial companies and were beginning careers as designers and ceramicists. It was fascinating to see the incredible diversity of the pieces on display. There were some beautifully simple and delicate items that almost looked as if they had been made of paper, while across the room were some really large plates and bowls decorated in a myriad bright colours. Each range was not just the product of the artist's hands but of their thoughts and emotions too. Here were statements of belief about the nature of beauty and its relationship to functionality and I was reminded of the old Shaker maxim to have nothing in your house that is not both beautiful and practical.

Our world is full of beauty – beautiful people, beautiful views, beautiful words and music, natural beauty and beauty that is the product of human imagination and skill. Discussion and debate rages about what or who is most beautiful. The search for beauty is pursued in a million different ways, admired in a million different ways and marketed in a million different ways. It is, of course, big business and is therefore so easily cut off from its roots and exploited for a commercial return. Our presuppositions about beauty are consequently prone to manipulation, our imaginations easily directed by photographers, designers, architects, city planners and artists who shape our visual surroundings and determine the way we see the world. Our view of the world is subtly edited.

Some beautiful things impact us profoundly and immediately take our breath away by the naturalness of their beauty. Yet there are other things, sucked into our consciousness by our eyes, which, although producing a similarly stunned response, are the product of somebody else's ideas about beauty rather than our own. Beauty is very much in the eye of the beholder but our eyes have been conditioned to see beauty in particular ways. The fashion industry is the most obvious example. Styles of clothing that nobody would have been seen dead in one year before are suddenly filling the high street stores and selling. Magazines talk about 'this season's colour'. A well-placed designer label can convince many consumers that an article of clothing previously considered out of the question may be exactly what they were looking for. This is just one example of the way we are conditioned to see beauty. And before any us of tries to climb onto the moral high ground and point out the extravagant vanity of the consumer, or the immorality of the sweat shops where much of this clothing is manufactured (all of which is certainly valid), remember this: beauty is a vital part of creation. In Genesis 1, on five occasions (Genesis 1.10, 12, 18, 21, 25), God judges his creation to be 'good' and on one occasion (Genesis 1.31) he pronounces creation to be 'very good'. When the Bible records this, it is not recording that God believes creation to be morally good, but to be aesthetically good, pleasing to the eye, beautiful to behold and lovely to see. In fact it would be reasonable to translate these six verses, 'And God saw that it was *beautiful*.'

Beauty is a vital part of creation. Beauty enriches our lives, and the lack of it (often without our noticing) leaves us impoverished. The problem so many of us have is that our search for beauty has become too restricted and too predetermined by the opinions of others. As a result, we recoil when we see somebody who doesn't conform to our preconceived notion of beauty, somebody with a disability, somebody with cerebral palsy who can't control their dribbling, somebody with a prosthetic limb whose movements are jerky, a person with the facial characteristics of Down's syndrome. We might admire such people, we might like them, but we struggle to find beauty in them and consequently we deny them a piece of their humanity. It was once said to me that in Italy all girls are told they are beautiful when they are growing up. I don't know if that is true but I hope it is, except that I would want to take it a step further and say that boys should be included too. All boys and all girls, able bodied and disabled alike, all should grow up knowing that they are beautiful.

Of course, I don't really expect anyone to disagree about this. It is, after all, rather like apple pie and motherhood, universally affirmed as 'A Good Thing'. But it doesn't happen. People are not told that they are beautiful. Many people, maybe most people, have no sense of being beautiful. They may believe themselves to be gifted in other ways but certainly would not see themselves as beautiful. I have to confess at this point that I do find the makeover programme *What Not To Wear* fascinating. I like the way the presenters believe that everybody is beautiful and that all they need is the right clothes to bring it out. The issue here is time. It takes time to get to know somebody and until we make that investment of time we will never get beyond superficial beauty, we will never shake off the glasses given to us by a world that predetermines what we look for and persuades us to conform to very particular notions of beauty. The more we spend time with people, the more beauty we see in them.

The problem with all this is not simply to do with vanity or positive self-image but the way it affects our understanding of creation and even, therefore, the way we think about God. Disability, if we are not very careful, draws out from us a mistaken theology that says material things, things of the earth, are bad, even evil, and need to be escaped from. It is easy to appreciate why this line of thinking should develop, even become comforting. If you are struggling to manoeuvre a wheelchair through a world full of obstacles, or trying to participate in a conversation with the hearing community, or trying to make sense of a world run by NTs,[11] then there are a great many reasons for considering that the things of the earth, on the whole, are a nuisance. If you are worn out, if you are taken to a place of mental and physical exhaustion that you thought existed only in your night-mares – by the daily routines and pressures of being a carer, or by disillusionment with the material world, its intolerance, injustice and prejudice – it is understandable.

However, Genesis 1 is insistent that the world as God sees it is good. It is insistent that God's instinct towards the world is first and foremost to bless. The response of many will, of course, be to say that the world forfeited this right to God's blessing as a result of the fall, and that from the moment Adam and Eve ate the forbidden fruit the world was no longer good. This view, I believe, is simply not upheld by scripture. I intend to look at creation 'post-fall' in the next chapter but a number of points can be made here.

First, the creation story of Genesis 1 was written down in the first instance for the benefit of those Israelites in captivity in Babylon in the sixth century BC. That is not to say that the narrative does not have earlier origins, but the context of the story as we now have it was that it was written for those who, with their world in tatters, were questioning their identity, their purpose and their God. It was written for a group of people who had serially ignored God's word as spoken by the prophets and was written to affirm the hope that Israel's God had not been defeated by the gods of the Babylonians. Yahweh remained the giver and ruler of all life. In other words, disobedience had not precluded blessing. The story also 'cuts underneath the Babylonian experience and grounds the rule of the God of Israel in a more fundamental claim, that of creation'.[12] The creation story was written to affirm God's ongoing intention to bless. The first people who would have read the story as we now read it were struggling in exile. As Brueggemann says:

It continues to be ground for faith in this God when more immediate historical experience is against it. Its affirmation is this: God can be trusted, even against contemporary data.

> The refutation of contemporary data may include sickness, poverty, unemployment, loneliness, that is every human experience of abandonment.[13]

To Brueggemann's list we could also add disability. God still sees this world as the place to which life and love can be given, a place that remains good and beautiful despite the parallel presence of evil. In the ministry of Jesus we see this affirmed: 'For God so loved the world . . . Indeed, God did not send the Son into the world to condemn the world, but in order that the world might be saved through him' (John 3.16–17). Furthermore, we see in the ministry and teaching of Jesus a sea change in attitudes towards the disabled. No longer are they seen as the objects of God's wrath and punishment but are now held up as central to the Kingdom of Heaven, even heralds of the Kingdom of Heaven. The crippled, the lame and the blind are called to the heavenly banquet. The man born blind, says Jesus, is not disabled as a result of sin but in order to become a walking advertisement for the work of God so that through his life others will come to know Jesus as the Light of the World.

Jesus is the pre-existent Word of God, the agent of creation. What he does in his incarnational ministry on earth is entirely consistent with the role he played in bringing all things into existence at the beginning of time. God takes us further. The claim of the narrative is that God fully intends to go on working in and through the creation, through the things of the earth and the fabric of the world. This world is the place where God's purpose and will is to be ultimately fulfilled. When Christian spirituality becomes disembodied or dematerialialized and makes out that physical stuff is necessarily bad, it descends into something more like Gnosticism.

This has the inevitable effect of producing a system of belief that is more dependent on the observance of religious law than it is on blessing, more oriented around rules and ethics than it is around grace. Beauty calls forth grace and emphasizes blessing. In making the world beautiful, God is seeking to evoke deep passion in his creation. In its beauty, the world is also attractive. (This, of course, was part of the problem with the Garden of Eden. It was almost too easy for the serpent to tempt Adam and Eve because everything looked so positively divine, including the forbidden fruit.) We are attracted by creation's beauty because it reflects the beauty of the creator himself, and as such this beauty reveals the creator's desire to draw creation to himself and to maintain a relationship of intimacy. At the beginning of time, the themes of intimacy, tenderness and dependency, which are summed up in the phrase 'and God saw it was beautiful', are established. They are themes that will resurface again most profoundly in the Song of Songs and then in the life of Jesus. They are themes that call us to a radically different approach to living. They call us to compassion. The further we become detached from creation, the less compassionate we become. The loss of any meaningful sense of being dependent beings, living in response to the beauty of God, results in the hardening of our hearts.

As well as taking on himself the sin of the world, Jesus also took on himself the ugliness of the world. The prophecy of Isaiah describes what would, and did, happen to the Messiah:

> He had no form or majesty that we should look at him,
> nothing in his appearance that we should desire him.
>
> (Isaiah 53.2)

By fulfilling this prophecy, Jesus could be said to have dealt with ugliness in the same way that he dealt with sin. He could be said to have beautified the world once again. Why is this important? Because, as John O'Donahue points out, 'we have become obsessed with self-improvement and analysis. Beauty offers us refreshment, elevation and remembrance of our true origin and real destination.'[14] O'Donahue recognizes that we so easily lose sight of our need for inspiration that our imaginations need stirring occasionally, that we need something awesome to kindle hope and aspiration. Our response must be to allow beauty to soften our hearts, to point us beyond ourselves so that we never forget that we are dependent creatures. Jesus refers to himself as the Good Shepherd (John 10). The word for 'good' is in fact *kalos*, a Greek word that might better be translated 'beautiful'. Jesus is the Beautiful Shepherd, the one who seeks to identify beauty in his sheep and draw it from them. The beauty he creates in us runs much deeper than glamour, image, personality or good looks. As the Beautiful Shepherd, he wants to inspire us and lift our vision of what we might become.

To spend any time at all in the company of those who have disabilities is to discover to our shame that beauty, like God himself, is not always to be found where we think it is. We need each other if we are to penetrate the mysteries of our humanity. We have a tendency to honour and celebrate only those who have highly achieved, who have risen to the top, whose success is measurable. But what statement have we made in the process? Jean Vanier says this:

> There is a lack of synchronicity between our society and those with disabilities. A society that honours only the powerful, the clever and the winners necessarily belittles the weak. It is as if to say: to be human is to be powerful.[15]

One of the people most celebrated for being powerful, and rightly so, is Admiral Lord Nelson. Standing magnificently on top of his column in London's Trafalgar Square he is the very epitome of heroism. He is also disabled. His one arm and singular eye are just as famous as his naval victories. Two hundred years after the battle of Trafalgar, another statue of a disabled person was also placed in Trafalgar Square. Known as the fourth plinth, it caused a great deal of controversy because the statue was of the British artist Alison Lapper who was born in 1965 without arms and with shortened legs, the result of a medical condition called phocomelia. The statue also shows her to be eight months pregnant. It is a stunningly beautiful piece of work carved out of white marble by Marc Quinn and it stands 3.55 metres high. Its unveiling was surrounded by massive media interest and the public were asked for their opinions. 'I think there should be statues of disabled people,' was one response, 'just not here.' But the juxtaposition of the fourth plinth to Nelson's Column is, I would suggest, a masterstroke that compels us to redefine both heroism and beauty. The beauty of this statue calls us to a quite different approach to heroism, equally as inspirational as Nelson, and possibly more accessible. God has made and enjoys beauty. The beauty he calls us to discover now is beauty that will be fully revealed in the new creation.

Blessing

It is a terribly sad fact that human beings have a propensity to reject and exclude others. Think of the Holocaust, think of Rwanda, think of Northern Ireland, think of the bullying that takes place routinely in a high proportion of British schools. Tragically I meet so many people who feel that the

Church has excluded them. I think we have to be honest about this. I think we need to look honestly at ourselves, amend our attitudes and move forward. It does no good to hold endless inquiries. There are at least two causes for our rejection and exclusion of others.

The first is that people who are different from us, particularly people whose lives are, outwardly at least, more chaotic than our own, make us feel uncomfortable about the mess under the surface of our own lives. When we meet somebody with a disability we don't know what we will say to them, we get embarrassed because we don't know how to react, and we become anxious in case we are asked to do something beyond our comfort zone. We become aware at some level of our own limitations. When I am out with a group of our son's friends we get stared at a lot. It's all rather messy. Physically and emotionally it's messy and we would sooner have things neat and tidy.

Second, people are often rejected and excluded because deep down we believe that they represent a challenge to us in the battle to secure for ourselves, our families or our communities a plentiful supply of the world's limited resources. This is seen most dramatically in the debate about immigration and in the wars fought to gain control of oil, but it is also played out with great intensity at our daughter's primary school at Friday break time when the tuck shop opens. The fear of going without, of being left behind, of being disadvantaged runs deep.

Against this backdrop God says to us in Genesis, 'I want to bless you.' He does not say, 'Clean up your act and then I will bless.' He does not even say, 'Your blessings on any given day will be proportionate to the moral quality of your lives.' While the Bible, starting in Genesis, makes clear that our actions have consequences, God retains the right (maddeningly) to bless whomever he pleases and withhold blessing from any he pleases. The question is, does this make God capricious or quixotic and his creation random and unreliable as far as justice is concerned? These are important questions for those with a disability. Genesis 1 lays down this principle: all human persons seeking to be made whole in the image of God cannot at the same time be graspers, control freaks or serial manipulators. The Garden of Eden is set up so that human beings have a choice to make. You can live in one of two ways, says God, you can live by grasping or you can live by my blessings. You can live a defensive, hoarding life, or you can live lightly and freely. You can live primarily to ensure your own interests or you can recognize that life is a gift and live to serve. This is what the forbidden tree represents and I want to come back to it shortly. The forbidden tree stands in the garden and gives humans a choice: attempt to *be* God, or choose to live *dependently* upon God. This forbidden tree is placed in the centre of the garden and it represents the central choice of our lives. But let us be under no illusions about this: in a world that gives little away, it is a very tough choice to make.

God sets Adam and Eve in the garden and gives them a vocation. Genesis 1.26 and 1.28 says that God intended them to 'rule' or 'have dominion' over creation. In Genesis 2.15 God says, 'till it and keep it.' In some translations this reads, 'work it and take care of it'. These injunctions suggest a gardener or a shepherd is to be the primary human vocation. The concept of exploitation is certainly not implied in the word 'rule'. In fact, the words here rather imply that God wants human beings to serve creation, to bring it to fruition, to steward it lovingly. Take the story of Ruth.

Naomi and Ruth herself leave Moab after the death of their husbands and return to Naomi's home town of Bethlehem. With nobody to provide for them, Ruth goes out into the fields and gleans the grain left over by the harvesters. This was a practice prescribed in the Law of Moses:

> When you reap your harvest in your field and forget a sheaf in the field, you shall not go back to get it; it shall be left for the alien, the orphan, and the widow, so that the LORD your God may bless you in your undertakings. (Deuteronomy 24.19)

The Genesis principle is clearly evident here. Work the land, bring it to fruition, but don't be a grasper in order that God may bless you.

This same principle emerges again and again throughout the Bible. Do you want to see God's blessing of healing? Then look at the prophet Isaiah who spoke the following words:

> Is not this the fast that I choose: to loose the bonds of injustice, to undo the thongs of the yoke, to let the oppressed go free, and to break every yoke? Is it not to share your bread with the hungry, and bring the homeless poor into your house; when you see the naked, to cover them, and not to hide yourself from your own kin? Then your light shall break forth like the dawn, and *your healing shall spring up quickly*; your vindicator shall go before you, the glory of the LORD shall be your rearguard. Then you shall call, and the LORD will answer; you shall cry for help, and he will say, Here I am. (Isaiah 58.6–9; italics mine)

God's blessing comes when we have the courage to live for others, particularly the poor and the marginalized. The reverse of this is illustrated in a parable told by Jesus in Luke 12, which, it seems to me, translates into our contemporary context very easily. An entrepreneur was very successful. He was so successful he did not know what to do with all the wealth he had created. So he said to himself, I will simply stash it all away and then live the good life for years to come. But God said to him, 'You fool, tonight your life will be demanded from you and then who will get their hands on your wealth?' That is where the parable ends, but what I want to know is this: what did he die of? Maybe a heart attack brought on by the stress of a life driven by the need to get rich? What was said at his funeral? Maybe there was grudging admiration for his achievements, but was there any real love? I know how easy it is to get into the habit of accumulation. My wife and I used to live in Nepal. When we came home to England all of our worldly possessions fitted into two barrels. When we moved into our current house we required two enormous lorries to transport all our things!

So you can live in one of two ways, says God: you can live by grasping or you can live by blessing. Actually, Genesis is saying to us that only one of these ways is really living and that is the way of dependency on God. One of the projects that I have had the privilege to see in action in recent years is based in the slums of Delhi that house around 4 million of the city's 14 million people. Asha, which means 'hope' in Hindi, was founded eighteen years ago by Dr Kiran and Freddy Martin and works to improve slum conditions and bring desperately needed health care to some of the world's poorest people. The quality of sanitation, water provision, housing and health provision has risen sharply as a direct result of this inspirational work that is now, rightly, achieving international recognition. Babies are no longer dying of preventable diseases; children are being given access to computers; corruption and intimidation of the poor are being challenged. Much of the success of this work is attributable to the *Mahila Mandals,* or women's groups. These women, many of whom have lived much of their lives as virtual slaves, are now empowered and organized into formidable teams of lane volunteers (each looking after a narrow slum alleyway) and community health volunteers who oversee the medical needs of their communities with passion and great pride. When I walked down the narrow, shanty town alleyways of Anna Nagar and Tollitpuri and half a dozen other slums, I was shown a plethora of child immunization cards by excited mothers of healthy babies. In a country infamous for the largest number of maternal deaths in the world, only one pregnant woman died in Asha's slums out of nearly two thousand antenatal cases in 2005. The comparison with the slum colonies where Asha is not working and where open sewers, ill health and disease are prolific is profound. But Asha's work is characterized not only by physical improvements. The women's groups are also places of passionate prayer. They know that even the best organization in the world is going to have a hard time making any sort of difference in a slum colony in Delhi. They know that they depend on God and on his ability and desire to bless them and see their communities transformed. They pray expectantly for miracles and they see God's Kingdom coming. They are completely committed to community transformation and to the health work that they do, but they know that ultimately they live by being dependent upon God's blessing.

The fruit of all this is remarkable. A once despised and abused section of society has found dignity. Police officials, who once regarded the poor as little better than animals, now offer them tea when they call to discuss community matters. Slum lords, more used to extortion and exploitation, now seek the advice and counsel of the *Mahila Mandals.* Although massive problems still remain, amazingly, the human propensity to reject and exclude has, in these profound ways, not been allowed to have the last word. Courage, faith and compassion have brought new life.

I am firmly convinced that this principle applies equally in the area of disability. So often disabled people are excluded from the everyday things of life because they can't keep up, can't contribute or can't understand. Out of a commitment to greater efficiency (frequently a euphemism for grasping), we perpetuate a godless status quo and say that we will rely on God's blessing at another time or in another place. Sometimes it would appear that the world of disability is like a parallel universe where the opportunities, pace and anxieties of life are completely different to everybody else's. A father of a boy with severe cerebral palsy expressed to me his anger (about which he felt guilty) that resulted from another father worrying about their son not getting straight A grades at GCSE. 'Didn't he realize', he said, 'what I would give for my son even to be able to take GCSEs?' If we want to learn how to live dependently upon God's blessing we need to bring these universes together and spend time with those who help us get beyond our deep fear of being human, who help us see our lives differently, and who make us realize that while free-market economics may have delivered much, it is still fallible and there is a place for not harvesting to the edge of our fields.

Rowan Williams points out that until around 1700, there were social rituals that formalized the notion that charity, which had then a much wider meaning, was a good thing. Charity, he argues, has now become something of a lost icon, not that charitable acts no longer take place, but that we have lost the understanding that charity is important for social cohesion because it emphasized that all are equal in the sight of God. He writes: 'Charity is bound up with the spirit of carnival, in the sense that it challenges any assumption that we are, as human beings, committed first and foremost to victory in the battle for material goods.'[16] He later goes on to say:

> Charity ultimately begs the question or poses the presupposition that behind the equalising of status, the development of social respect, the invention of social ritual, is an attempt to cope with a set of unchosen truths about the universe, and ultimately with the most comprehensive fact of all, the dependent condition of the universe and everything in it.[17]

Where are the places that we go to learn about being dependent? Amazingly, despite the fact that information technology has made the world so much smaller, we have become more fearful of those who are different because now we need only communicate with those who are the same. God's command to us remains the same: depend upon me. Until we stop pulling up the drawbridge on those who are different and instead live out that commandment with compassion, we will cut our world and ourselves off from the source of primary blessing.

Boundaries

There is something quite frightening about being human. We are easily threatened. Our insecurities and neuroses, at least the ones we are aware of, become our travelling companions through the years. We find it difficult at various times in our lives to escape the terror of loneliness; not the passing indignity of being left off somebody's invitation list, but a deeper loneliness that leaves us wondering who on earth we

48

are. It was this deeper, existential, loneliness that characterized Adam and Eve after they had eaten the forbidden fruit.
Intimacy and security were replaced by distance and fear. It
was this deep loneliness that Jesus was addressing when he
said to his disciples, 'I no longer call you servants, now I call
you friends.' Adam and Eve suddenly became outsiders,
Jesus' policy of friendship is about establishing a doctrine of
inclusion. The fear of exclusion is at the heart of so many
human problems and it began when Adam and Eve over-
stepped the boundary that God had given them. We have
an odd relationship with prohibitions and boundaries.
The prohibition that God established in the Garden of Eden
was put there for a purpose. It was put there so that Adam
and Eve could enjoy the garden as it was intended and
for the purpose of fruitfulness. The prescribed pattern of
behaviour was designed to enhance human freedom, not to
curtail human rights. God does not want human life to be
fearfully lonely.

However, once the forbidden fruit is eaten, the human
response is to hide from God. Why? 'I was afraid,' said
Adam. This fear not only damages the human's relationship
with God but also damages inter-human relationships, and
the human relationship with the rest of creation. Instead
of harmony and trust, we now have, for the first time, hier-
archy and the need to control. Real anxiety has now entered
the world. Here is the origin not of sin or evil (the text is
rather vague about these abstract ideas) but of the human
need for strategies of survival that orientate existence not
around God, or the God-given vocation to be shepherd or
gardener, but around the self. 'I was afraid . . . I hid . . . I was
naked,' says Adam. These strategies for survival lead fairly
directly and quickly into 'oppressive social relationships and

to authoritarian and hierarchical ways of organising life'.[18]
It is such approaches to life that have turned disabilities
into handicaps. What started out as a limitation (disability)
subsequently also becomes a barrier to accessing the ordinary
things of life (handicap).

I came across the following moving example of the way that
parameters for 'normal' behaviour can so easily be imposed
in a way that is life-denying rather than freedom-enhancing.
Autism is one of the most difficult disabilities to address,
so wide is the extent and range of the spectrum of issues that
come under this one umbrella. In *Joe: The Only Boy in the
World*, a devastatingly honest account of his own son's condition, Michael Blastland describes one encounter with a
child psychologist:

> Joe, aged three or four, was seated on a tiny chair at a tiny
> table while a psychologist perched on an equally small chair
> opposite. Slowly, deliberately, the psychologist produced a clear
> plastic cylindrical tub with a lid in which there were three holes:
> round, square and triangular. Parents everywhere will know
> them. He removed the lid (a mistake), emptied half-a-dozen
> shaped wooden blocks onto the table and replaced the lid. Next,
> the obvious test: taking one of the shapes between finger and
> thumb with the deliberation of a magician, fingers splayed, a
> dainty touch and a raised eyebrow, he showed us clearly how
> to push it neatly through the appropriate hole. It clattered
> into the tub. Presto, he smiled, and pushed the remaining
> shapes towards Joe. Joe pulled the whole tub closer, slipped
> off the lid, which he tossed onto the floor, and began plop-
> ping shapes straight in. Less stage craft, admittedly, and, oh,
> alright, less precision too, but my, what efficiency!
>
> Only, no, sorry, the psychologist was not testing for that.
>
> 'Joe! Joe!' he interrupted through the plonking blocks, 'let
> me show you again.'

Something in the rules of the test forbade spoken instruction. Joe had to watch, learn and repeat. He watched as the man poured out the pieces, which Joe liked, watched as the man demonstrated his magic again, and then repeated exactly what he'd done first time, flipping off the lid and chucking in the first of the shapes.

'No, Joe,' said the man, taking away the toy.

Joe, however, didn't care for no. He thought 'yes', the pouring out bit was most interesting and he wanted it again. He thought it quite insistently, in fact, and I have to say I agreed, though not perhaps with quite Joe's vehemence, as the two of them became locked in a tussle for control of the tub. I smiled inwardly . . . impressed by Joe's directness: stuff the prissy malarkey with the holes, let's do the noisy, jumbly bit. Joe, meanwhile, was being failed.[19]

Being failed is one of the big issues within the disability world. Our own son Ben will take every opportunity to play cricket. While the rest of the family loved our visit to India, the one redeeming feature of India for him was the fact that everyone plays cricket. When he was a little younger, and we spent most summer holidays in Cornwall, he would spot a game of beach cricket miles away and scuttle off to ask if he could join in. Invariably people were very kind and invited him to play but you could tell that they were not expecting him to be able to hit the ball. I used to enjoy the moment when Ben's turn came to bat and the fielders would be fishing the ball out of the sea! He actually has a good eye for the ball. However, he is still not as able as most children and could just as easily get out first ball. In the highly competitive world of beach or park cricket there is little forgiveness. If you are lucky, there will be a rule that you cannot be out first ball, but nothing can be taken for granted. I can remember one such cricket match, when my back was turned for a moment but I was near enough to hear a batsman getting out, followed by a sickening thud, a second of complete silence, and then deep wailing. I turned to see somebody else's child with a huge egg over his right eye screaming, 'Ben hit me', and he meant with the cricket bat. From that moment on I realized that before Ben could join in any games of cricket it had to be explained to the other children that Ben would need to play by different rules. He would need to be given twelve balls to bat which he could use up regardless of whether he was out or not. At the end of these twelve balls, he would let the next person have a go even if he was still in. It often took a while for the other children to see the sense in this. Why, they thought, should there be one set of rules for one person, and another set of rules for everybody else? I am convinced, however, that in the end these highly competitive children enjoyed the experience more. Somehow they had been given permission to access a different part of their own personalities. They had learned things about themselves that would have remained unlearned. They had discovered a different way of relating to others that was not simply about domination. Maybe, I sensed, some had even begun to learn how to survive their own failures and they exhibited a degree of relief that there was another way other than the way of win at all costs. That does not mean to say that all elements of competition were removed, far from it, there was still an intense desire to do well, but somehow the atmosphere had changed and a different set of values prevailed. I have seen this happen during a number of cricket games but still have rarely felt relaxed enough to leave everybody alone to get on with it. The memory of the sickening thud and the bulging eye, as well as one or two other similar if less dramatic moments, prevent me from being entirely confident that all is now Utopia in the world of informal cricket. The way of inclusion is no soft option.

The story of Joe, as well as our own experiences with Ben, highlight for me the way in which we create boundaries, parameters and norms of behaviour that speak volumes about our own insecurities and fears of being human. When we read about the boundaries that God established in the Garden of Eden we are still tempted to conclude, as were Adam and Eve, that God must be some petty despot if he wants to deny us access to such crucial information. But when we have the courage to allow part of the game to be played by different rules and parameters in order to facilitate inclusion, the result is often that everybody discovers a new freedom. It might even be said that the original (God-ordained) purpose for parameters is recovered: that is, that human beings could rest secure in the knowledge that God wanted to bless them. 'Remember the widow, the orphan and the alien,' declared the Law of Moses; 'I have not found such great faith in all of Israel,' said Jesus on encountering one remarkable Gentile. Some people with disabilities will feel that they want no special allowances or rules to be made for them and that is fine. However, whether inclusion is brought about as a result of changing legislation or changing attitudes does not matter. Inclusion is God's desire and intention. Inclusion is the resource God has given us to release one another into freedom. Our fear of being human, our very real anxieties about the responsibilities of inheriting what God wants to give us, are continually exploited in public life by media and marketing executives seeking to draw arbitrary lines around certain groups of people, deeming them to be desirable, and inviting the rest of us to aspire to belong to such groups, when the very act of doing so requires us to leave behind and reject those who have the capacity to bring freedom into our lives.

Genesis 1 contains many themes that are relevant to our understanding of ourselves. I have looked at just three. I hope that reflecting on these from the perspective of disability means that we can learn to get beyond the common limitation of partial vision and become more fully alive to the possibility that in the breaking down of boundaries between people we can rediscover the original, God-given boundary that allows us to be fully human and God to be fully God.

4

Which way now?

One of my favourite church services of the year is the Mencap Service. There is always a lovely atmosphere, it is not unusual to find the visiting preacher becoming a little emotional during his or her address, and there is among the families of those with learning disabilities and among the carers an unspoken understanding of the peculiar lives that so many live as a result of living with and caring for a person with learning disabilities. It is an important event because there are very few occasions when people with learning disabilities occupy the central role. For most of the time they are expected to adapt to what everybody else is doing and manage the best they can on the periphery. The most important thing is that the presence of God is very tangible. During one of these services, a young woman with Down's syndrome, called Kirsty, arrived a little late and walked up to the front where my wife was sitting. She had her recorder with her. I was leading the service but she pointed to me and said to my wife, 'I want to speak that man.' A moment later I sat down. 'I'm going to play the Sky Boat Song,' she told me. I quickly looked at the service sheet and, although I wasn't sure if she could play the Sky Boat Song, I thought we could make space for it at the end of the service as a meditation and a time to think about what God had been saying to us in the service. So after the last hymn, with some trepidation, I announced how the service would end. Kirsty duly played her piece, which she did very well, and called over to the organist to play the final voluntary. Then she bowed and sat down. It was clear that Kirsty had badly wanted to play the recorder in the service and I was pleased that there had been the opportunity for her to do so. She was also quite assertive and determined. It would not have been easy to stop her playing.

Afterwards I was thinking about Kirsty's contribution to the service. I was pleased that she had been able to take part as an equal; there had been no sense of the token disabled person now having the floor. But fundamentally she fulfilled a desire that is basic to all of us, but which remains unfulfilled in the majority of people, that is, the desire to have a role. Without a role to play we struggle to know our identity. Without a role to play we find it difficult to form meaningful relationships. Without a role we get disillusioned and easily suffer from low self-esteem. In our mad and busy world it has become rather fashionable to find ways of escaping from 'doing' and instead to concentrate on simply 'being'. I am totally in favour of silence and contemplation and advocate this approach to faith in these pages. But the contemplative tradition fully embraced leads us to being better equipped and enabled to fulfil our responsibilities in the roles that we have in daily life. The contemplative tradition helps us to understand ourselves better so that we can see more clearly when we are hanging on to certain roles for the wrong reason or not accepting other roles that God is offering us. Often in the Church we give our roles another name, *vocation*: discovering our own purpose in life.

The problem with limitations

One of the by-products of a consumer-driven society is that we begin to believe that it is somebody else's responsibility (or role) to make us happy. I'm paying for it, therefore I ought to get it. It's all about what other people can do for me. The desired objective or purpose of so much of life, the summit of so much sad ambition, is consequently to have no role at all. Meaningful vocation is found in service, usually sacrificial service, but the concept of living sacrificially has been lost today under the onslaught of a prevailing belief that proclaims that we are all entitled to everything. Possibilities, we have come to believe, are limitless. Freedom and fulfilment are found by jettisoning everything that limits or restricts. Disability is therefore a profound challenge to contemporary living because those who are disabled keep insisting that a fulfilled life is possible within the limitations that a particular disability imposes.

Many people with disabilities find it extremely difficult to convince others that fulfilment is just as much a real possibility for them and are often denied the opportunities to achieve their potential on account of the low expectations of what it is perceived they can achieve. Many children are aborted in pregnancy on the grounds that a congenital abnormality will impose too many limits on their future life for fulfilment to be a genuine possibility. The Church also needs to recover confidence in the message that it is *only* within limitations that our real vocation, purpose and role can be discovered. The problem is that this sort of approach does not sell very many self-help guides.

Vocation has always been central to identity. I looked in the last chapter at some of the many things that were original

in creation: original vocation (humanity's calling to steward-
ship and shepherding); original beauty; original blessing;
original boundaries. I want to turn now and look at the one
original that seems to fixate us most, the one thing in fact
that is most commonly prefixed by the word original, which
is, of course, original sin. The question is this: in what way
was the purpose or vocation of humanity affected by the disobedience of Adam and Eve?

Theologians have discussed at length the episodes that
follow Adam and Eve's expulsion from the Garden of Eden:
the accounts of Cain and Abel, the genealogy of the 'sons
of God', the Flood, and the Tower of Babel. These episodes
constitute what is called primeval history, the time before
the Patriarchal narrative begins with the calling of Abram
in Genesis 12. A number of different possible themes and
patterns in the text have been proposed.

1   Human sin – Divine speech – Divine mitigation – punishment

This is seen played out in the story of Cain and Abel in Genesis
4. Cain kills his brother Abel in a fit of jealousy in verse 8.
In verses 11–12 there is a divine speech where God pronounces
judgement. There is, however, mitigation for Cain when,
in verse 15, God undertakes to protect him from those who
would seek to kill him by placing a mark upon him. But in
verse 16, Cain still has to leave the presence of the Lord and
goes to live in Nod, east of Eden. This pattern is played out
five times in the primeval history of Genesis 1—11.

2   Spread of sin – Spread of grace

Throughout the five central episodes of Genesis 1—11, the
rift between God and humanity grows ever wider and more

cataclysmic. 'There is a movement from disobedience to murder, to reckless killing, to titanic lust, to total corruption and violence, to the full disruption of humanity.'[20] While God responds to all this with punishments that grow in severity, he also extends to humanity divine grace. Adam and Eve do not die, Cain is protected, the human race is preserved through the descendants of Noah.

3   Creation – uncreation – re-creation

Genesis 1 tells of creation being spoken forth from the watery chaos. It speaks of the separation and distinction of different parts of creation, of order being established and purpose being given. However, in the account of the Flood depicted in chapter 6, all is once again returned to watery chaos and only Noah and his family survive. Then, as the flood waters slowly subside, God reissues to the survivors instructions similar to those he first gave to Adam and Eve: multiply on the earth, be fruitful, increase in number. The separation of sea and land is once again established and the different species of animal are released again to roam the earth. The first creation is undone but God then resolves to re-create once more.

All three of these patterns highlight both the way in which humanity brings calamity into creation and the way in which God tries to steer things back on to the right track again. To look carefully at the text is to realize that this is no caricatured story of God playing a type of cane-wielding headmaster who summons recalcitrant human beings into his divine study with the words 'This is going to hurt me more than it hurts you', before administering the inevitable punishment. The Bible in fact starts, and subsequently goes on, by portraying God as giving purpose and vocation to humanity and, right from the outset, portrays humanity as struggling to embrace that purpose as its means of fulfilment. Almost from the beginning of humanity's time on earth, the Bible suggests that God's grace, blessing and goodness are not accessed when human beings achieve a certain standard of perfection but, thank goodness, when we have messed up and need it most. At the beginning of God's dealing with us, perfection is not the qualification for relationship with God. Reading only to the end of the first book of the Bible, this becomes clear. Noah, after the Flood, revealed another side to his character when he got naked and drunk; Abraham laughed at God's suggestion that he would father a child; Moses was a murderer; Jacob was a liar; Joseph was so conceited that it is possible to have some sympathy with his brothers' desire to get rid of him.

However, human beings, it would seem, have an insatiable desire for perfection, to look the best and be the strongest. It is not surprising therefore that people who do not conform to our ideas of human perfection are often considered to be less able to embrace or express a God-given vocation. It is commonly assumed, for example, that an intellectual disability is a handicap to beginning and sustaining a relationship with God. Why? Why are people with physical disabilities so often discouraged from pursuing vocations to full-time ministry in the Church? We very often seem to work under the premise that because human beings have limited ability, God also has limited ability. 'We can't, so God can't' is the motto for many Christians. We are so very slow to grasp that it is in the frustration of human limitation that God's grace is often most powerfully revealed.

So, what is the consequence of the sin that Adam and Eve committed? St Paul makes an important distinction when thinking about our human limitations. He recognized the difference between life *in* the flesh and life *according* to the flesh. Life in the flesh, or recognizing human limitations, which Paul saw as a vital Christian insight, was remarkably characterized in his own ministry by the way that, in Paul's own life, the awesome and miraculous acts of God unfolded alongside severe hardship and suffering. Acts 27 is a wonderful example. Paul was at this stage a prisoner being taken by ship for trial in Rome. A terrible storm blew up. For fourteen days and nights nobody on the boat had seen the sky. Most of the contents of the ship's hold had been thrown into the sea in a desperate attempt to stay afloat. The only thing that prevented disaster and death were the words of prophetic instruction that God gave Paul for the soldiers and crew of the ship. Finally they reached the safety of the island of Malta, but no sooner had they scrambled ashore than a venomous snake bit Paul. To the astonishment of all who were witnesses, Paul simply threw the snake off and into the fire. Paul then prayed for the father of the island's chief official, Publius, who was healed of fever and dysentery. Luke, the writer of Acts, goes on to record how word got out about this unusual individual and how every remaining person on the island of Malta who was sick took advantage of this turn of events and came to Paul. All were healed. The hardship and suffering of imprisonment and shipwreck co-existed alongside the awesome works of God.

So, based upon his own experience, Paul made the important distinction between life in the flesh and life according to the flesh. Life in the flesh is about recognizing our human limitations and finitude. It is about acknowledging that we are not perfect and that we depend upon the grace of God. Life according to the flesh, on the other hand, is essentially living for ourselves, for our own pleasure and gratification. Adam and Eve were tempted to live *according* to the flesh and it has been this temptation that human beings have had to come to terms with ever since. The human task, as first the book of Genesis and subsequently the letters of Paul outline for us, is to embrace life *in* the flesh. When we do we will realize that we are all in the same boat, all of us seeking to find meaning, perspective and help within the confines of limited bodies, minds and imaginations. This is the case for the able-bodied person who believes themselves to be self-sufficient, for the physically disabled person who feels that they have to try harder and succeed better, and for the intellectually disabled person of whom little can sometimes be expected. The biblical blueprint for God's people, from Adam and Eve, to St Paul and to us today, is that hardship and suffering co-exist alongside the awesome and miraculous acts of God. All of us have to come to terms with life in the flesh. All of us have to come to terms with the Lordship of God. All of us have to embrace our limitations. This is an understanding that ought of necessity to prompt us to release disabled persons (as well as any others on the margins) into full participation in the life of the Church and the ministry of the Kingdom of God.

The recognition of our limitations has led to some of the most innovative designs of recent years. Take, for example, the cordless kettle. This was originally designed for people who had problems with manual dexterity. Now, however, kettles in the majority of kitchens are cordless kettles. What started out as a piece of specialist design has been recognized as good design for everybody. In the world of motor cars, look at the Ford Focus, the best-selling car in the United Kingdom. This was the first car to be specifically designed with the less mobile in mind, yet it has also won awards and sold in vast numbers because its design works better for everybody. These examples of so-called inclusive design demonstrate that when we are inclusive in our thinking, when we recognize that we are all in the same boat, that we are all struggling to live in the flesh, then we will collectively find a more constructive future.

The invisible Kingdom

So what is it that prevents us from embracing what for St Paul was a self-evident fact of life? It may have to do with the rather obvious truth that the Kingdom of God is an invisible Kingdom. Throughout his public ministry Jesus was constantly asked to give a sign, to establish an opposition to Roman rule, to give some physical proof. But at his trial before Pontius Pilate, Jesus made it clear that his Kingdom was not of this world but from another place. In the Church today we are often still tempted predominantly to seek after physical and visible evidence of the arrival of God's Kingdom rather than things that are invisible. Throughout a great deal of church culture, physical healing and prosperity have a greater significance than the resolution of equally detrimental problems such as greed, prejudice and hardness of heart.

Where does this leave disabled people? A Church that has swallowed the world's desire for visible proof, and has little or no room for an invisible Kingdom, is going to be, consciously or unconsciously, in a muddle about the place of disabled people who visibly and physically present both practical and theological problems. Rather too much Christian living is a misguided attempt to avoid living in the flesh rather than avoiding life according to the flesh. It is therefore little wonder that so many people leave the Church, finding its practices of little help to life in a material world. If everything on the Church's agenda is an attempt to make the invisible visible and available for all to see, there will be few points of contact between the message preached and the life that is experienced. If we can only talk about a God who reveals, and remain silent about the God who sometimes conceals, can we offer any hope to the vast majority of Christians (and others who sincerely seek) who spend periods of their Christian lives wondering why they have lost touch with God? Maybe those of us who are standing at these various crossroads simply need love and reassurance that the Kingdom of God is not of this world but is still at hand; that it is invisible but it is still present; that it is not all about solving our problems but about revealing to us a way of living within our human limitations, and addressing the deeper, spiritual powers and authorities that grip the world.

The process of judgement

Living within our limitations is therefore important, but it is not the only implication of Adam and Eve's transgression. The book of Genesis states that humanity now also had to come to terms with judgement, a concept that any post-modern society running along according to the principles of liberal democracy finds particularly hard to understand and embrace.

Philip Yancey retells a story from the Bible that greatly puzzled one of the Church's greatest theologians, St Augustine.

The story comes originally from the Gospel of St John (chapter 5). Jesus was in Jerusalem for a feast of the Jews. As he was entering the city at the Sheep Gate he saw what was probably a familiar sight, a crowd of disabled people gathered by the pool of Bethesda. Sometimes the water of the pool would be stirred up. What followed was the pitiful sight of the waiting crowd crawling, limping and hobbling over the stones to enter the water. One of these people had been there for thirty-eight years. He was so disabled that throughout all that time he had never once been able to get into the water. Jesus directly and simply said to him, 'Get up! Pick up your mat. Walk!' At once the man was cured. Obviously this was a marvellous result for the paralysed man, but it is not the end of the story.

> Jesus then slipped away into the crowd. He ignored the rest of that great throng of disabled people, leaving all but one unhealed. Why? Augustine wondered: There lay so many there, and yet only one was healed, whilst he could by a word have raised them all up.[21]

Later, Jesus found the same man at the Temple. This time what he said to him also begs more questions than it provides answers: 'See, you are well again. Stop sinning or something worse may happen to you.' Is Jesus implying that in some way the man's thirty-eight years of disability had been caused by his own sin?

Those familiar with the Gospels will know that Jesus often linked forgiveness of sins with acts of healing, but, paradoxically, Jesus also taught that sickness was not the consequence of sin. So, for example, when Jesus was asked whose sin had caused a certain man to be born blind, he replied, 'Neither this man nor his parents sinned' (John 9.3). At one moment it would appear that Jesus is tying sickness and sin together, but the next moment he seems to be offering the radical teaching for his day that they are not to be considered as cause and effect at all. Would we be right to conclude that there is something contradictory in these aspects of Jesus' teaching?

It is worth pointing out that in these acts of healing Jesus seems to be implying that he wants to go beyond mere physical healing to the altogether deeper level of making the subject whole. Such a work would necessarily also imply forgiveness of sins. However, contained in Jesus' desire to forgive sins is the concept of judgement. Jesus takes sins enormously seriously. Sins provoke judgement, which then leads to two further consequences: forgiveness and punishment.

As we have seen with Adam and Eve and the primeval history of Genesis 1—11, these two things proved not to be mutually exclusive. The Greek word for judgement is *krisis*. In her book *Face to Face*, Professor Francis Young, herself the mother of a severely disabled person, makes the important point that very often disability does indeed constitute a crisis in the life of an individual or a family. She sees the obvious link between the English word 'crisis' and the Greek word *krisis* as having significance. When a crisis, such as coming to terms with disability, occurs, it reveals what is really going on in the deep recesses of our lives. Our responses, our attitudes, our fears, our prejudices are all exposed by the beam of a scouring searchlight that leaves no area of our lives in the dark. Such an experience can be deeply troubling. We are faced with who we really are. Such a crisis is, therefore, also a moment of *krisis*, a moment of judgement. It is a moment of judgement because it reveals to us how well we are doing in the task of embracing the vocation God is giving to us, how well we are doing at living by grace within our human limitations.

I once watched a television documentary about three soldiers all badly wounded in the Iraq war. One soldier had been horrifically burned, one had lost a leg and one had suffered a nervous breakdown. The programme-makers also interviewed their families and asked how they had coped with the trauma of seeing a loved one in such pain. Both the soldiers themselves and their families spoke with moving honesty about the struggles they had been through and the ways in which they were facing the future. All were trying, without a shred of self-pity, to rebuild ordinary lives. The maiming effects of war, the trauma in two of these cases compounded by the fact that their injuries had been caused by friendly fire, and in the third case by serious lack of understanding, was a massive crisis that seemed to bring out huge reserves of strength from them and their families.

A friend of ours who has a daughter with Down's syndrome has spoken of the days immediately after Emma's birth. The people who visited them seemed to fall into one of two categories. Either they would say, 'God has really blessed you to give you a child with Down's syndrome, they're just like angels.' To which the stifled reply could so easily have been, 'Well, shall we ask God to bless you in the same way then?' The second group of people would say something like, 'Isn't it awful how the devil just sneaks in like that.' As a new parent of a child with severe learning disabilities this is equally unhelpful as it leaves you feeling that you are bringing up a child under a banner that might just as well read, 'Of the Devil!' We were thinking about the cards we received when Ben was born. All were kindly meant but many would have been more appropriate for bereavement.

These stories of soldiers returning home and of parents with disabled children are all examples of the way in which a crisis reveals what is really going on in an area of our thoughts and inner lives. We all live from the inside out. The peace, fulfilment, confusion or neuroses that exist within us will come out and be displayed in our public lives whether we like it or not. Jesus said that it is not what goes into a person but what comes out of a person that determines whether or not they are clean or unclean. He had harsh words of judgement for the religious establishment and said they were like whitewashed tombs, respectable on the outside but inside full of dead bones. Judgement works on many levels. We are called as Christians to take judgement seriously but without being judgemental in our attitudes to others. We have to hold together the sayings of the same Jesus who said both that he was not sent to condemn the world (John 3.17) and that it was for judgement that he had come into the world (John 9.39). It is only in Jesus that judgement does not have to imply condemnation.

It is the common experience of people with disabilities, and their parents or carers, that they are always being judged. We know so many parents of children on the autistic spectrum who are thoroughly disapproved of because their children are perceived to be out of control. Many people with physical disabilities spend much of their time and energy correcting the value judgements that others have made about them and their abilities. Many people with disabilities feel that hidden attitudes exist which conspire towards lower expectations of them in the first place. Is this oversensitivity on a grand scale? An excess of 'political correctness'? Or is it recognition that fairness and justice are requirements within the Kingdom of God and that the crying need of the Church is for discipled people growing into wholeness and holiness through the process of being aware of and shedding such prejudice, addictions and phobias in the light of Christ? This process of growth is also called sanctification and is another element of Christian life that is both invisible and long term and therefore not always given prominence. It is, however, of critical importance if the Bride of Christ, the Church, is to be ready for the arrival of the Bridegroom.

Nevertheless, Jesus seems to imply a further act of judgement on the man by the pool he has just healed in John 5 if he does not stop sinning. What does Jesus mean? Is there something that he wants this man to stop doing or saying or thinking, or is he asking something altogether deeper? David Runcorn writes this:

> When we define sin solely in terms of wrong actions or thoughts we trivialise it. Our diagnosis does not go deep enough. The problem is more radical and fundamental. Jesus furiously castigated and mocked the religion of his day for its pedantic obsession with external standards of behaviour. Who we are always comes before what we do. Our choices, desires and actions will always flow from our sense of personal identity. Our deepest need is not primarily to stop doing or saying bad things. The power and significance of sin lies not so much in what we are doing or saying but in who we think we are.[22]

I wonder if the challenge that Jesus presented to this healed cripple was that he should stop thinking of himself as the religious establishment had told him to think, namely as a hopeless and unworthy sinner, and accept his real identity as a child of God, healed, forgiven and accepted. I wonder if this is not the challenge that Jesus presents to all of us.

Think back again to Adam and Eve. Their undoing lay in the fact that they believed what the serpent said to them. 'God knows', said the serpent, 'that when you eat of it [the forbidden fruit] your eyes will be opened, and you will be like God, knowing good and evil' (Genesis 3.5). Adam and Eve became convinced that they could indeed be like God. Think of the temptation of Jesus in the wilderness. The first thing that the tempter said to Jesus was, 'If you are the Son of God . . .'. It was a direct challenge to the affirmation that Jesus had so recently received at his baptism when a voice from heaven had affirmed his identity with the words, 'This is my Son, whom I love, with him I am well pleased.' The Bible seems to suggest that the root cause of sin, the place of greatest temptation, is not so much the things we say and do, but the mistaken ideas we have about who we are. For many disabled people it is an ongoing struggle to find a place of acceptance, a place of opportunity, where such biblical identity can be forged. Perhaps we need to see judgement as more of an ongoing process of growing into maturity together. After all, we often view salvation as a process. We talk about the fact we have been saved, that we are saved, and that we will be saved. Perhaps judgement too is a process, those moments of crisis/*krisis* that occur throughout life, providing the opportunities to be more completely healed of the obstacles that prevent us from receiving the fullness of life promised by Jesus, helping us to know what exactly we are saved from. It is a process that the Bible says will culminate in a final judgement, but by that stage it is also clear that few destinies will be left undecided.

To speak about judgement then in the context of disability is to break the cause-and-effect understanding that disability (or in fact any sickness) is a consequence of sin. What is sin, and therefore open to judgement, are the attitudes and practices that prevent people from inheriting the identity that God wants to give to everybody.

What or who fell in the fall?

Genesis 2, the account of Adam and Eve eating the forbidden fruit, is commonly held up as the ultimate point of origin for all that is bad and evil in the world. It is therefore frequently assumed that it must also be the point of origin for disability. The further assumption is then also made that the new creation, of which more later, will see the eradication of disability because all that is bad or evil will, of course, disappear at that point. However, are these safe assumptions? What exactly is Adam and Eve's moment of disobedience all about? Walter Brueggemann makes a number of introductory comments about the way that this part of the Bible has been treated over the years.

First, he points out that the Bible itself does not seem to regard the story of Adam and Eve as a pivotal narrative which controls the way we should read the entirety of scripture. Rather, no further reference is made in the Old Testament to the story of Adam and Eve and it is only in the early chapters of Romans that the story really achieves further prominence. Even in Romans, Paul is not attempting to construct a particular anthropology. Brueggemann points out that, within the Bible, the story of Adam and Eve has only marginal importance and that, largely due to St Augustine, we have lost this sense of perspective.

Second, Brueggemann asserts that the narrative cannot be treated as an account of 'the fall'. In fact, he says, the Old

Testament does not really assume such a fall. There are also a number of other Old Testament texts where the people of God are similarly given a choice to follow God or reject God, Deuteronomy 30.11–14 being a good example. The story of Adam and Eve is only one such story among many others. Again, it is not until much later in the unfolding of the Old Testament, when we start to hear the prophecies of Hosea, Jeremiah and Ezekiel, that it becomes justifiable to construct a more pessimistic view of human nature.

Third, the story of Adam and Eve is often believed to be an explanation of how evil came into the world. However, theologians have always found that such questions of theodicy (the study of the origin of evil) have no easy conclusions. This story, along with the Old Testament in general, does not intend to give a neat answer for how evil came into the world. It is not concerned with such theoretical issues. Rather, the text seeks to address itself to the much more practical question of how human beings go about living faithfully to God in a rebellious world of perversions, temptations and abuse of power. This is not to say that the Bible dismisses the reality of evil; but it does not seek to give answers to abstract questions about its origins so much as to give guidelines as to what to do about it.

All this leads to some important conclusions. If Brueggemann is right, and other commentators do agree with him, then we can no longer conclude that disability had its own genesis at the moment when Adam and Eve ate the forbidden fruit. It becomes possible to suggest that there was no world before Adam and Eve's moment of disobedience that was disability free. It might even be possible to go further and say that the world that God looked at and saw was so good was in fact a world that already, quite intentionally, contained what we now call disability. If the assumption that Genesis 2 is the definitive account of the origin of evil is to be questioned, the further assumption that the presence of disability is linked to the events in the Garden of Eden is even more flakey. Thus the link between evil and disability, which Jesus destroys in the Gospels, is seen entirely as an ancient human construct having little or no foundation in scripture.

Furthermore, if disability was present in the Garden of Eden, or at the beginning of time when God saw that all was good, then it must have been present in such a way that was pain free and prejudice free. In fact, it could hardly have been described at such a moment as 'disability' at all. I find such a picture of Eden to be deeply attractive. I see here real affirmation and fulfilment for the people I know and love who have disabilities. I see here the potential for removing the stigma that is attached to so much disability. I see here a blueprint for human dignity that was always God's intention right from the start.

The book of Genesis portrays the world as reluctant at best and rebellious at worst, unable to embrace the purposes of God. It makes clear that this has consequences for humanity. What seems to have happened, however, is that we have somehow arrived at the misunderstanding that these consequences are much more far-reaching for a disabled person than for the rest of us. The fall, judgement, human weakness, we appear to believe, are far more serious for the disabled than for the rest of us; they have taken the brunt of it. In one sense this is true but maybe it would be more accurate to think that it is not God's line of fire that they have accidentally strayed into, but ours. Our disobedience to God has resulted in us losing sight of God's intention for balance, harmony and unity. Those now consequently known as 'the disabled' are the ones who end up pushed out. In the new heaven and the new earth, which are to come, God intends to get back to some Eden principles.

5

So what's new?

A friend of ours attended a retreat at a well-known retreat centre and, when she got there, discovered that the main programme was being run by and for the deaf community. Undaunted, she joined in with some of their meetings and in conversation with them she said she thought it was wonderful that in heaven they would be able to hear again. Actually, came the reply, God uses sign language! Some other friends of ours who have a very bright son with severe cerebral palsy said to me that they believed that Benjamin would still have cerebral palsy in heaven, but that it will no longer be a handicap to inclusion and fulfilment. Indeed, when I think about our own son, if I believe as I do that God knew him before he was born, knitted him together in his mother's womb, that Down's syndrome did not slip in when God lost concentration or was looking the other way, then Benedict is no mistake and logically God would not want to remake him as a different person for the purposes of heaven. However, this assertion leads to the very legitimate question: so what's new? What will be different about heaven if all these disabilities are still present? And if the reality of heaven ought to influence our lives now, in what way should that influence shape us in the present?

Before addressing these questions, it is important to differentiate between congenital disabilities that a person is born with and disabilities that affect a person either at birth or later in life. Not only are there emotional differences in coming to terms with a disability that you were not born with, but there is also the obvious theological difference. A person who becomes disabled at a specific point in their life can hardly be said, theologically or biologically, to have been formed that way during their mother's pregnancy. In an important sense, the question, 'Why has this happened to me?' is then answerable in different ways. It may be because of a medical mistake. It may be because of an accident. It may be the consequence of illness such as a stroke. It is impossible for a person with an acquired disability to say that they were created that way for a purpose. Within our own family, our son Benedict was born with Down's syndrome, while my wife Jackie became disabled as a result of illness. Jackie was not knitted together in her mother's womb with a malfunctioning left leg in the way that Benedict was knitted together in Jackie's womb with Down's syndrome.

What we are assuming with these questions is that the best way for anybody to understand their identity is to do so from the point of view of eternity. Christians do not, however, believe that we have to wait until we get into the dimension of eternity, the new heaven and the new earth, before we can start to participate in eternity's reality. Jesus came preaching the good news of the gospel, telling people to repent for the Kingdom of Heaven was at hand. In other words, we believe that, secretly and silently, the Kingdom of Heaven is already present now. It is clearly far from fully present and there is much discussion in the Church about the extent of the Kingdom's present reality and about its implications. There are obviously times and places where God's Kingdom seems very close, and other moments when it still seems so very far away. Looking at all this from the perspective of our current study, we might previously have been tempted to assume that wherever disability is present, because of all its attendant struggle and difficulty, the Kingdom of God would be at its most distant. I hope that we have all begun to appreciate that the opposite might be true. That we can very often catch vivid glimpses of eternity, of God's Kingdom breaking through into the present moment in the form of answered prayer, faith being shared and communities and churches transformed, through the ministries and lives of people with disabilities. What we need to do, therefore, is to be more aware of what kingdom activity looks like so that we can better spot its presence.

When the Kingdom of God arrives, individuals respond in faith

A variety of things can happen when individuals respond in faith to the arrival of the Kingdom. A consistent theme, however, is that people find themselves set free from their past. They are no longer victims of past events but have been given a new life. Henri Nouwen describes this process as a journey in which one moves from fatalism to faith.

> We are always tempted with fatalism. When we say, 'well I have always been impatient, I guess I'll have to live with it,' we are being fatalistic. When we say, 'that man never had a loving father or mother, you shouldn't be surprised that he ended up in prison,' we speak as fatalists. When we say, 'she was terribly abused as a child, how do you expect her to ever to have a healthy relationship with a man,' we allow fatalism

to overshadow us . . . Fatalism is the attitude that makes us
passive victims of exterior circumstances beyond our control.
The opposite of fatalism is faith.[23]

The response of faith has an immediate practical effect. One
of the buried questions that anybody facing disability has
to ask is this: how much do I want to come to terms with
this traumatic situation? What reason do I have to get on
and live an ordinary life? This is a buried question because
it is hidden underneath years of emotional debris that con-
tributes for so many people to low self-esteem and poor
self-image. For people who acquire a disability, this is particularly tough. If you felt worthless before becoming disabled
it is very difficult indeed to find the inner resources to say
effectively both to the world and to yourself: do not consider
me a lesser person now that I am disabled. If you already
considered yourself to be a lesser person, the onset of disability is very likely to compound any such negative self-
understanding. How does the perspective of heaven impact
a person in such circumstances? It could lead to resignation,
to the thought that maybe I'll just have to wait until I get to
heaven for things to improve, or it could lead to the thought
that as I'm not going to be redundant in heaven, neither will
I be redundant now! This is the response of faith, a response
that God himself helps us make.

When the Kingdom of God arrives, the community of faith becomes inclusive

Most societies, organizations and groups throughout history
have struggled to welcome outsiders and have frowned upon
individuality and difference. Conformity is what the majority

of establishment leaders have wanted. Look at education, for example. Esther De Waal writes about an early experience in her teaching career:

> Having never before taught in a school and given a free hand, I chose to study the archaeology and architecture of the city (of Canterbury). One afternoon having taken them through the roof spaces of the cathedral I set them their homework: to write about the experience and tell me what they had seen. The reaction was one of anxiety and dismay – they were used to copying out from their text books or to writing notes on some set topic, but to tell me what they had seen in the amazing space they had just been exploring, to express the relationship of vaults, ribs and bosses, the range of arch and pillar, the play of light and shadow, left them totally non-plussed.[24]

It is not only schools where we seldom encourage independent thinking and imagination and where we find it hard to welcome difference of approach; the Church has been wrestling with exactly the same issues for centuries. I talked in an earlier chapter about the place of boundaries, the means of defining what is acceptable and what is not. Leaving aside for a moment some current contentious debates and discussions surrounding orthodoxy (correct thinking and doctrine), let us look instead at the issue of orthopraxis (the right way of doing things). The problem is that so much of what we think constitutes orthopraxis excludes people with disabilities. Singing hymns, for example, is very problematic for the deaf community. I would also contend that when we get our orthopraxis sorted out, much, if not all, of our orthodoxy could be ironed out as well. So what does our understanding of heaven's arrival tell us about the right way to go about being church?

When the Kingdom of God arrives, the Church will be increasingly multi-sensory

The first thing that strikes me in this regard is that heaven is a multi-sensory area. There are vivid descriptions that dramatically describe what Jesus will look like in Daniel, Ezekiel and Revelation. There is a huge range of sound. Sometimes it seems to be quiet and reverential, sometimes loud, and sometimes the noises will be those of a party merrily taking place. And if there is a heavenly feast that we are to share in, then it seems likely that there will be things to taste. It is a physical place and there will objects to be touched and people will probably embrace one another. There will be the smell of incense. It is described as a place of movement, as the saints, the angels and the majestic heavenly creatures live to worship God. Heaven is truly a multi-sensory area.

It is widely recognized that as human beings we have seven senses: sight, movement, hearing, taste, smell, touch and something that occupational therapists call proprioception, which, I am told, is the sense of where you are in space so that, for example, if you closed your eyes you would still be able to touch the end of your nose with your finger with a good degree of accuracy. Those who are familiar with the world of learning disabilities will know that multi-sensory areas play a very important role in stimulating children and adults alike. And in reality all of us have a preferred sensory approach to encountering the world and learning about it. Some of us have a disposition towards accessing things in an auditory way, some of us are touchy-feely people, some of us take in the world around in a clearly visual way, and so on.

However, much of the way that church is organized and worship is done requires everybody to have a strong auditory approach to life. Other senses are frequently not needed. I am no longer convinced that this adequately reflects the heaven that awaits us, or gives our mission in the world right now a good platform for success. It certainly means that many people with disabilities stand little chance of encountering the God who loves them. Probably, though, it is not only the disabled community who are excluded. It is anybody who is not an auditory person. I wonder what the impact would be on the life of our nation if our church buildings became multi-sensory areas? Compliance to the Disability Discrimination Act only touches the surface. There is so much more we could do in the life of the Church to engage the interest of more people if we took our senses seriously. It would, however, deeply challenge what happens in our church life.

A friend and neighbouring minister has a church situated near a residential home for people with learning disabilities. About half-way through most Sunday morning services a group of people arrive from this home to join in the worship. On one occasion, a large globe had been placed near the altar that was to be used as an aid for praying for the needs of the world. One of the recently arrived worshippers, a man probably whose dominant sense is that of movement, saw this globe and promptly went up to the altar to investigate. Then, rather like Charles Atlas, he proceeded to pick up the globe and wave it above his head at the front of the church. Having now become rather excited by this activity, he went on to flick 'V' signs to the rest of the congregation for a few minutes before finally taking his seat again. The wonderful thing is that nobody tried to stop him. Nobody took offence. Nobody really batted an eyelid. Here was a man simply allowed to be himself in church. What a fantastic example of orthopraxis allowing flexibility and a glimpse of heaven.

When the Kingdom of God arrives, human activity should become less frenetic

The new heaven and the new earth are God-made not human-made. This might seem a really obvious statement to make but let me quote Dallas Willard: 'The greatest temptation to evil that humanity ever suffers is the temptation to make a "Jerusalem" happen by human means . . . the intrumentalities invoked to make "Jerusalem" happen always wind up eliminating truth, or mercy, or both.'[25] Willard recognizes that humanity has a vital role to play in the unfolding of God's plans on earth. We are called to action and what we do matters to God. Ultimately, however, it is God who creates the new heaven and the new earth, as the prophet Isaiah prophesied in Isaiah 65.17–25. What are the implications for this?

One of the key components to missiological thinking at the end of the twentieth and beginning of the twenty-first centuries is the idea of contextualization. This is the notion that in order to make the gospel relevant, in order to enable people to see that God is alive today and speaking into the world, the historic, orthodox message of faith must be repackaged in a contemporary way that is appropriate to a specific cultural context. This understanding has been one of the most significant ideas learned by the Church in the last twenty years. It has been a key principle in the success of the Alpha course, for example, and has helped thousands of people to find faith in Christ.

However, not even good missiological method is able to bring about the new heaven and the new earth. Only the initiative of God can do this. The principle of contextualization, while delivering much, can lead to an expression of church life that simply replicates popular culture and leaves us alienated from people different to ourselves. Young people minister to other young people, white people to other white people, and so on. I wonder if somewhere along the line we have lost sight of a previous, but no less central, principle to mission, that of crossing cultural barriers. And, if this is the case, we will also have lost sight of the very positive by-product of this process, that as we cross cultural barriers we learn invaluable lessons about ourselves and gain a fresh understanding of God.

The importance of this to issues surrounding disability is that in many ways the world of disability also has a culture all of its own. It has its own language (sign language); it has a myriad of different support groups, associations and networks; it has a very particular set of needs. It is, in a great many respects, a world of its own. Sometimes I learn the signs for a particular song or hymn we are going to sing in church in order to get the whole congregation involved in using the signs to sing in a different way. I explain that we are not doing a children's song with actions but are using proper signs, a different language. The reaction is always interesting. About half the congregation join in and enjoy the experience and about half look embarrassed and are unable to participate. This may have something to do with feeling awkward about being asked to use their bodies, but it could also highlight just how difficult many find it moving into a different culture. Among those who did feel able to participate in the signs, many tell me later of the profound impact it had on their ability to enter into God's presence in worship. I always use signs when leading worship where the majority of people present have learning disabilities, and others who also come along at these times are frequently moved to tears by the depth and sincerity of their encounter with God by worshipping in this way. For me it is a reminder that the new heaven and the new earth are a gift from God, not something that evolves through human effort. There is, interestingly, more universal approval for the use of signers standing at the front of church meetings to accompany the words of songs or sermons.

This 'other world' that is the world of disability, this culturally different place from that in which most of us live, has huge riches to offer those prepared to cross this particular cultural barrier. The consequence of successfully managing this experience is the dawning of the realization that God is so much bigger than the projects and programmes that I thought were indispensable to my own small space, and that it is God, not I, who will bring about the new heaven and new earth. This in turn serves to place increasing emphasis on renewal of church life and a fresh hunger for things of the Holy Spirit, particularly spiritual gifts.

When the Kingdom of God arrives, we will be characterized by diversity

The first Pentecost was truly international and, with church trends being what they are, it might be wise to expect the new heaven and new earth to be populated mainly by people with an earthly origin in either China or Africa. There will be huge diversity of historical and geographical backgrounds, but there will be unity of purpose. As well as the saints of God, there will also, of course, be angels and other heavenly creatures such as cherubim. The key to the roles we will have in heaven is not the status or fame that we may have achieved on earth but the faithfulness we have displayed in whatever Jesus has called us to on earth. We could see this as the replacement of 'political correctness' by a new phenomenon: 'heavenly correctness'. The prominent personalities of heaven will, in many cases, have been utterly obscure while they were on earth. They will have been considered as marginal people and of marginal importance. Many, I believe, will therefore be from the disabled community.

Again, I wonder whether it might not be a good idea to start practising heavenly diversity in our churches now to reflect what will come into being in the future. This could start with the way we recruit new ministers in our churches. Advertisements for new ministers can betray a trend towards homogenization and convey a sense that a church wants more of the same when recruiting a future incumbent. Often 'someone like us' is sought, preferably a minister with a young family to attract other young families. This despite the fact that Jesus seemed to make a priority of attracting misfits and marginal people. It is so easy to be churlish and cynical in portraying such caricatures, and I have no desire to be so, but I would love to see an advertisement for a new minister that said something along the following lines: 'St Botolph's has realized that as we are all of much the same age and colour, we would like our new vicar/minister/priest to be entirely different from us so as to attract different people, possibly even unusual people, to our church. We would like our new woman/man to love God passionately but all varieties of external appearance will be considered.'

Many will no doubt argue that it is most important to maintain continuity and stability when making appointments, either because the world around is changing so rapidly or because a certain model or tradition of church has seemingly proved fruitful. Perhaps some would also argue that I have missed the central point to the incarnation, namely that Jesus became just like humanity, not different from us, in order to fulfil his purpose on earth, that, in Anselm's words, he became like us so that we could become like him. And yet the reason that Jesus angered so many was that he challenged the norms of his world; he appeared to be, and was, like any other person in society but made outrageous claims that he was also different; and he exhibited powers that enabled him to do what nobody else could do. The crowds, in fact, followed Jesus because he was different and not like other teachers and rabbis.

How do we deal with difference? Such a question is obviously of considerable importance to people with disabilities. How do we relate to people whose ways are not our ways and whose thoughts are not our thoughts? How do we work out which of our attitudes or patterns of behaviour are central and indispensable to the life which God has called us to, and which are merely the products of culture? I am suggesting here that the approach Christians might take in addressing this question is to look at things from the perspective of the future as it is shown to us in the Bible. We live now in preparation for what is to come, the new heaven and the new earth, and although there is much that necessarily remains mysterious about these things, we do know that there will be no more death, or mourning, or crying, or pain. Thomas Merton said that what we do now is practice for what we will do in heaven; therefore the things we do now are acts of hope. Hope brings heaven into the present.[26] Dealing with difference in the light of these questions therefore becomes an eschatological issue. That is, we believe that we should live in the light of the coming Kingdom of God, which is both here at the present time but also still to come in the future. Philosopher and novelist Iris Murdoch maintained that the end of her novels shaped the beginning, and in the same way the end times should shape the way we live now.

When the Kingdom of God arrives, things will start to be made new

The end times, as the Bible portrays them, are cataclysmic, seismic events. The Bible's imagery is vivid and dramatic.

> But in those days, following that distress, 'the sun will be darkened, and the moon will not give its light; the stars will fall from the sky, and the heavenly bodies will be shaken.' At that time men will see the Son of Man coming in clouds with great power and glory. (Mark 13.24–26)

However, these dramatic happenings will then be followed by the renewal of heaven and earth.

> Then I saw a new heaven and a new earth; for the first heaven and the first earth had passed away, and the sea was no more. And I saw the holy city, the new Jerusalem, coming down out of heaven from God, prepared as a bride adorned for her husband. And I heard a loud voice from the throne saying, 'See, the home of God is among mortals. He will dwell with them; they will be his peoples, and God himself will be with them; he will wipe every tear from their eyes. Death will be no more; mourning and crying and pain will be no more, for the first things have passed away.' And the one who was seated on the

throne said, 'See, I am making all things new.' (Revelation 21.1–5)

This promise of God is vital to people with disabilities and to their families. I very frequently talk to parents of people with learning disabilities who have spent twenty years under huge stress and strain trying to hold a family together with a child with a learning disability, only to find that relinquishing the caring role, as a son or daughter moves into a care establishment or some form of sheltered accommodation, is even harder. Tears punctuate literally every day, for the death of hopes and dreams, and for the physical and emotional pain. In these circumstances it is so important to know that a time will come when God's intervention will bring all this to an end for ever.

It has been my experience, particularly during the two weeks of the year that I spend at the New Wine summer conference with people who have learning disabilities, that those who have been taken to the very end of themselves through caring, those who have become disillusioned with life, as well as others who did not even realize the extent of their own spiritual need, have consistently recovered this understanding and experience of the Holy Spirit as the first fruits of the promised hope that is to come and they have done so within the disability community. Those thought to be different, to have little by way of spiritual gifts, to be objects of care alone have become our spiritual guides and teachers. Let me tell you of a couple of people whose stories, I hope, demonstrate this.

Helen's story

The first five years of Helen's life were comparable to most people. But at the age of five, and for no reason that doctors were able to determine, Helen suddenly developed very high blood pressure which caused a stroke. Helen was unable to walk or talk and doctors said that she never would do either of these things again. Quite how a five-year-old could ever cope with such a turn of events is hard to imagine, but not only did Helen resolve to come to terms with her loss of speech and movement, she also determined that she would prove her doctors wrong – she would learn how to walk and speak again. She missed a year of school as a result of the stroke, the months frequently punctuated by regular trips to Great Ormond Street Hospital, and it was during this time that she learned that her condition was to become yet more complicated. Helen received the further diagnosis that she was suffering from neurofibromatosis, or NF. This is a condition that results in swellings developing on most of a person's nerve endings. As these swellings are close to the surface of the skin, the effect is to cover most of a person's body with lumps and bumps.

Helen did manage to regain the ability to walk but now she can only cover short distances with difficulty. She has recovered her powers of speech and talks very articulately about life as a disabled person. Her life has continued to have many ups and down. She has had many opportunities to dig deeply into the well of courage that is at the heart of her being. Feeling that there was something lacking from her life, she resolved to be confirmed at the age of sixteen. It was without doubt an independent decision and a moment of genuine Christian awakening. Shortly after, she moved schools. It was a bigger institution altogether. No doubt the staff considered themselves to be considerate and helpful. However, towards the end of every lesson, Helen was told to leave class ten minutes earlier than everybody else and ten minutes before the lesson was actually finished in order to avoid being late for the next period. Consequently, not only was work missed but every lesson of the day ended in humiliation. She was tired all the time and felt constantly that few people outside her family believed that her life had any purpose.

Her next school proved to be a much better experience and incorporated training for independent living alongside academic work. She felt able to offer herself for voluntary work and began to find fulfilling work in a charity shop. The charity's aims were to provide opportunities to help people with disabilities back into work. Everything began to look more positive. Helen represented the charity at a function given by the mayor of Bath. However, a couple of months later, somebody was sent from the charity's head office to tell Helen that, due to health and safety regulations, she had to leave the shop immediately. There was no farewell, no flowers, no card, no expressions of sadness about how things had turned out, just please do not come back.

Shortly after this, Helen was shopping in a newsagent's. Somebody saw her, they looked at her appearance and saw her mobility difficulty. Then they turned to her and said to her face, 'You shouldn't be here, you should not have been born.' It is shocking to write down such things as this. It is numbing to think that such words could really have been spoken. It is remarkable that, in the face of such terrible prejudice, Helen has constantly believed that she must simply get on with life and that God has placed her on earth for a purpose. She insists that it is her faith which has preserved her sense of being a valuable human being.

There have been moments of triumph as well. In her late twenties, Helen began tall-ship sailing. She has been up the mast (in her wheelchair) of a ship called the Soren Larsen,

the ship used in the filming of television's *Onedin Line*. She
has been abseiling, she has flown a microlite and been up in
a hot-air balloon. She has learned to ride a horse. She maintains that she is lucky to be as she is, that Jesus has taken
away the emotional pain inflicted by rejection and humiliation, and she wants to find opportunities to help others. Is
this a happy ending? Does Helen walk off into the sunset to
live happily ever after? The fact is that she remains disabled
and that she will, almost inevitably, face more prejudice in
her life at some point in the future. I asked her which was
a more difficult thing to confront, poor physical access into
a building or negative attitudes and preconceptions about
disabled people. She immediately answered that attitudes
and assumptions posed the greater difficulty as she seeks to
be included into ordinary life. I asked her if she considered
disability to be a product of evil. Again she immediately
answered, 'No!'

This is the common answer whenever I ask this question.
It is an answer that forces us to wonder what, then, is the cause,
philosophically, spiritually or religiously, of disability? If we
cannot use the easy answer that disability is caused by evil,
what in earth or heaven (these being the only two places of
origin left to consider) is it caused by? There is no ultimately
satisfying answer that I have heard expounded to this question but maybe it is a question that points us to the bigger,
more important, realization that the world does not always
seem programmed to run according to the laws of cause and
effect. Bad things do happen to good people. Wickedness does
sometimes bring prosperity. This, however, is not a reason
to abandon faith in a God of justice and goodness, but a
motivation to do what is good and holy for its own sake
and not for its immediate reward. Thomas Merton again:

'Christian life can reduce you to despair, and sometimes it is meant to. But giving your life to God is a theology of hope.'

There is much that is unknown about the new creation that Jesus promises to inaugurate, but there are, nevertheless, things that we do know. There will be no more mourning, sadness or tears; there will be total justice; there will be no handicaps. The first will be last and the last will be first; those considered least in the eyes of the world will be considered greatest in the Kingdom of God. Helen has taught me that hope and perseverance belong together. She is not a person to pity, she is a gifted woman whom God is using to build his Church. Considered from the perspective of heaven, Helen is a person of considerable stature.

Charin's story

Charin Corea was born on 3 February 1996 to Sri Lankan parents living in London's East End. His mother had a long thirty-six hours of labour during which time Charin underwent foetal distress. However, he walked early, showed great aptitude for reading ahead of time, and was generally thought to be a bright child. At eleven months he was given the MMR inoculation. He continued to thrive. At eighteen months he was talking fluently and his language was advanced for his age. But by twenty-one months everything had changed. No longer was there any language, nor indeed any eye contact with his parents. He simply turned inwards. He began lining up his toys in an obsessive manner. His behaviour became harder and harder to manage. The diagnosis soon followed of Pervasive Developmental Disorder, a condition more commonly known as autism.

What followed for Charin's mum and dad was a period of grieving and bereavement. The period of coming to terms with the arrival of disability, your own or a family member's, seems universally to impact every area of life. Relationships, career, leisure, finances, nothing is free from its effect and nothing can prepare you for it. Faced with so much to absorb, Charin's parents, Ivan and Charika, did what I remember we also did, and what so many parents do in similar circumstances, they sought to better understand what they were up against. They discovered that the most effective means of education for children such as Charin was a Picture Education Communication system (PECs). This system, however, was only available in the USA. They asked the Local Education Authority if it might be possible to bring PECs to Essex. The answer was no. Believing it to be the best way of educating Charin, Ivan and Charika decided to buy PECs anyway. They then also paid for the teachers at Charin's school to be trained in its use. The quality of the system has now been generally accepted and subsequently adopted across Essex.

Education has always been a difficult issue for Charin. He has been excluded from infant schools and junior schools. In his first Christmas at school he was prevented from coming inside for the Christmas play and left outside alone in a cold playground. The obvious irony seems unmissable: the infant Jesus was not the only child for whom no room could be found that year. Charin and his family have been thrown out of taxis and building societies because Charin simply cannot queue up like everybody else. His parents came to the point when they felt they had no choice but to attempt to change the wind. Their question was and is a direct and simple one: why should our son be excluded from all the everyday things of life on the sole grounds that he is autistic? Wherever exclusion takes place, it has become their policy, graciously but firmly, to challenge it. When Charin was around six years old he was taken to a well-known burger chain as a reward for making good progress at school. He was accompanied by his mum and two members of staff. When it was discovered at the restaurant that Charin was autistic, he was banned from playing in the children's play area. Charin's dad immediately telephoned the restaurant's manager. The manager was completely uninterested in what had happened. Ivan decided not to let the matter rest. He contacted the constituency MPs, both in the area where the restaurant was located as well as the constituency where the chain have their UK headquarters. He wrote to the restaurant chain's chief executive in England and in the USA. The MPs threatened to bring the issue to the House of Commons and the restaurant backed down. As a result, however, they now have a disability policy throughout the country and train their entire staff to be aware of the issues surrounding disability. Charin was offered a free burger.

The Corea family have brought autism into parliamentary circles in other ways as well. They became aware that nationally 520,000 people were diagnosed as being autistic and they wanted to raise awareness of the issue and educate people. They were at first apprehensive about what could be achieved by an Asian family from Essex, but during 2002 over eight hundred organizations came on board to support their campaign during a year that became known as Autism Awareness Year. They directly approached the Prime Minister for his support and on 5 January 2002 Tony Blair became the first parliamentarian to actually use the word 'autism' in the House of Commons since Leo Kanner first came up with the term in 1948. Later that day another MP, Linda Perham, sponsored a parliamentary debate on autism. Many MPs had realized for a long time that their mailbags were full of letters from people with concerns surrounding autism. Now at last it seemed that those concerns were being taken seriously. The Department of Health and the Department for Work and Pensions consequently both have policies for the fair inclusion of people on the autistic spectrum.

The Corea family have campaigned in four specific areas: education, health, specialist speech therapy and respite care. It is in these areas that the Government is now seeking to take policy forward. It would be easy to think that the everyday needs of people on the autistic spectrum will not really be impacted in any significant way by the bureaucratic machinery of Government, and it would be fair to say that good policy does not always result in effective grassroots change, but Ivan and Charika have now been invited four times to 10 Downing Street to discuss the implementation of Government policy. Theirs is surely a major contribution to the cause of integration and a very significant challenge to the evil of exclusion.

As with Helen's account, I again wonder if this is a story with a happy ending? The issues surrounding the upbringing of a child on the autistic spectrum have not gone away. In all probability, there will be further occasions when prejudice and ignorance will cause more upset. But there is also no getting away from the fact that Charin Corea, an eleven-year-old boy with autism, has changed lives and moulded society for the better. He has been the means of unveiling unjust structures and attitudes; he has caused people to re-evaluate their priorities; he has brought people together for mutual support who otherwise would have remained isolated; and he has influenced the most powerful person in the land. That, in my opinion, is pretty good going! It is, however, not the complete story. There is hanging on Charin's bedroom wall a picture of Holman Hunt's famous painting of Jesus, the Light of the World. He regularly prays to Jesus who he knows cares for him. In his prayers he says, 'Thank you, Jesus, for loving me. Jesus, I love you.' This is the same boy whose autism-inspired behaviour has caused him to be thrown out of schools, taxis and building societies; the same boy who seems to bring disturbance and love in equal measure, who is a walking microcosm of the beauty and brokenness that are the hallmarks of the world. Despite the fact that it has also been a struggle for Charin to be included in church life, he has been a catalyst for his parents' own deepening faith in Jesus Christ. Behind the bigger picture of campaigns and activism is the persistent belief that they are loved and that God has given their lives meaning.

Some Pharisees once asked Jesus when the Kingdom of God would come. He replied that the Kingdom of God is not something that can be observed, nor will people say, ' "Look, here it is!" or "There it is!" For, in fact, the kingdom of God is among you' (Luke 17.20–21). The Kingdom of God is subversive, it is invisible, it is easy to miss. It has not broken into the world by means of a form of heavenly coup d'état. The Kingdom of God does not arrive like the cavalry dramatically and in the nick of time. The Kingdom of God is already in our midst, or, as some manuscripts would have it, within or among you. We can either choose to believe it is present or we can choose to explain the existence of grace, of unconditional love, of the power of forgiveness, of broken lives healed and transformed, by referring to fate and fortune. What we cannot do, what to me makes no sense whatsoever, is to explain our existence in terms of getting what we deserve. This is one of the most unattractive assumptions of Western civilization. Theories from the survival of the fittest through to free-market economics, while delivering many important insights and advances, have left us with a legacy of belief that we are what we are because we are better than the rest. Some Eastern religions propound something similar in their doctrines of karma and reincarnation. But the suffering of the innocent and the prospering of the wicked demonstrate that, certainly in moral terms, we do not get what we deserve. Into this world, where we have had our own way for so long, a world that is in many respects more a reflection of our characters than of the character of God, the Kingdom of God breaks silently in. It is a Kingdom that is likened to a magnificent wedding banquet that in the end is bursting with the most unlikely guests: the poor, the crippled, the lame and the blind. In other words, Helen and Charin will be among the most honoured guests not me. If this is the case then I must learn from them now, while I have the chance, what life in the Kingdom is really all about. One day Jesus will return and then his Kingdom will be consummated.

Jesus told another parable that touched on the subject of his return. It concerned a widow who had been denied justice by a cynical judge. She, however, refused to accept the situation and kept pestering the judge, intimidating him with her determination. The judge even felt physically threatened by the widow, and so in the end he saw that justice was done. Jesus said that God would also grant justice to those who persist in prayer, but then he finished by saying, 'And yet, when the Son of Man comes, will he find faith on earth?' (Luke 18.1–8). Faith, as Jesus talks about it in this parable, is a powerful mixture of belief and action. The faith that the Son of Man seems keen on finding is faith of gritty character, that hangs on occasionally by the fingernails and is sometimes more about struggle than serenity. A colleague of mine was once going through a difficult time. God did not seem all that close. However, she resolved to take her dog for a walk and not return until she had counted one hundred ways in which God had blessed her. I believe it took quite a while but by the time the exercise and the walk were completed, perspective and peace had been restored. It has also been my experience that faith born of this kind of determination, this resolve to keep following Jesus even when life is unfair or difficult, produces genuine beauty in a person's life. I would have expected the opposite to be true, but time and again it is not hardness or bitterness that I see but beauty and grace and generosity of spirit.

But in the difficulties of simply getting through each day, how are we sustained and nourished in this hope? Paul's letter to the Romans, in one of the Bible's most important chapters, chapter 8, talks about the role that the Holy Spirit plays in keeping this hope alive. In verse 23, Paul says that 'we ourselves, who have the first fruits of the Spirit, groan inwardly while we wait for adoption, the redemption of our bodies'. The Holy Spirit's role as the first fruits of the new creation is one of his more neglected jobs, but it is vitally important. The Holy Spirit is given to us as a foretaste of all that is to come. It is as if God gives us a deposit and says to us that the best and the rest is still to come. Earlier in the same chapter, in verse 16, Paul has stated that we have already been adopted as God's children, that we are already co-heirs with Christ if we share in his sufferings. But in verse 23, Paul, almost going back on himself, talks about still waiting eagerly for our adoption, the fulfilment of that process. He talks about the way in which the Holy Spirit is given to us to keep that hope fresh within us day after day. Verse

24 goes on to say that it is in this hope that we were saved. People with disabilities and their families desperately need renewal of hope. It would probably also be fair to say that the Western Church is not usually characterized by hope at the present time. A series of ethical and doctrinal issues have contributed to discouragement. But to those who really need it, God gives an experience of the Holy Spirit as the first fruits of the new creation in order to renew hope and bring fresh vision and energy. Why? Because the Holy Spirit is a revelation, a glimpse, a foretaste of the perfect future that is God's ultimate intention.

And this is the point. Faith that has been fought for produces beauty. Faith that has been fought for acts as a magnet, it radiates the beauty of Jesus himself that is compelling for human beings. It points others towards the living water of eternal life. Consequently it is able to play an important role in the arrival of the new heaven and the new earth. We need to remember that the new heaven and the new earth will have aspects of continuity with this present heaven and earth, as well as aspects of discontinuity. David Bookless, talking about Christian responsibility towards creation, points out that in New Testament Greek there are two words for new, *neos*, meaning totally new, brand new, never been before, and *kainos*, meaning new as to form or quality, renewed rather than brand new. When the Bible talks about the New Jerusalem, or the new heaven and the new earth, or when it refers to God saying, 'Behold, I make all things new', the word used throughout is *kainos*. The implication is that there is to be continuity between this heaven and earth and the new heaven and earth. It is therefore not surprising that the Son of Man would want to find faith *on the earth* when he returns. He will be looking for it because those who have it will form part of the continuity between the old earth and heaven and the new earth and heaven and the establishment of the Kingdom of God.

In the end, there is simply too much that we cannot know about the new creation and we therefore cannot speak with any certainty about what it will hold for people with a disability. What we can, however, say is that everybody who is faithful to Jesus now will see the completion in their lives of all that God began to do on earth, and that the new creation itself will be able to accommodate with total justice and harmony a very wide range of people into a new community unified in the common theme of serving the purposes of God.

6

Compassion

————◆————

Any happiness which is built on being insensitive, in the retreat
from compassion, is ultimately unsustainable.

Timothy Radcliffe OP

There is an intriguing and well-known story that appears quite
early in Luke's Gospel, in chapter 5. It concerns four friends
and a paralysed man. The fame of Jesus had already grown
to such an extent that important teachers of the Law together
with community leaders had gathered from every village in
Galilee, Judaea and Jerusalem to hear what Jesus had to say.
The level of interest in Jesus was obviously huge. Many were
wondering if he was a prophet or even if he was the promised Messiah. The level of excitement was cranked up still
further by the elements of controversy that surrounded Jesus.
He did not seem to mind making provocative statements or
doing provocative things. He was very big news indeed.

But what of the four friends and the paralysed man?
Well, they had a problem. The level of interest in Jesus was
so high, and the crowds so big that, as they approached
the house where Jesus was speaking, it became very apparent that there was no way they would be able to get a
man on a stretcher in to see Jesus by normal means. So, two
thousand years before any form of disability discrimination

legislation required that architectural modifications be made to buildings, they embarked upon their own course of architectural adaptations and made a hole in the roof! It must have been a most dramatic moment. Starting with a scratching noise from above, then progressing to the sound of cracking plaster, then a cloud of dust, and then a shaft of sunlight spearing down into a gloomy, packed little room. The small hole then became a large hole and then the sunlight disappeared again for a few minutes as the hole was filled by the shape of a terrified man being lowered through the broken roof, convinced that he was going to be dropped at any moment. The property owner was probably not well pleased. The important teachers of the Law probably found the whole episode frightfully irregular. The crowd, I imagine, were loving the drama of the scene, and Jesus – well, I picture Jesus smiling up in admiration at the four people who had the temerity to stop at nothing, who were not going to take no for an answer.

The paralysed man was indeed healed in further controversial circumstances that involved his sins being forgiven into the bargain, thus infuriating the very important teachers of the Law, and delighting everybody else. The story concludes with Luke reporting the people saying, 'We have seen remarkable things today.' And they had. What, however, they had not seen, because they had been so busy getting front row seats at the Jesus meeting, was the moment when a couple of friends stopped on their way to the same meeting, maybe in the village market place or in a quiet alley, and called over to couple of other people to come and help them carry a man who was probably very well known to them, whom they had seen begging every day of their lives, whose condition they had simply taken for granted, whom they had walked past every day for years. But today they stopped, and I find it fascinating to ask why they stopped. I wonder why indeed anybody stops for another person in need. They then picked the man up. We don't even know if he wanted to go with them.

When, a few minutes later, they appeared through the roof above Jesus and presented the paralysed man to him, Jesus saw their faith, then looked at the paralytic and said to him, 'Friend, your sins are forgiven.' The gathered crowd may not have witnessed the moment when these four friends stopped to pick up the paralysed man, but I think that Jesus knew what they had done and I would like to offer the conjecture that Jesus had himself walked past that paralysed man on the way to his speaking engagement earlier that day, that he noticed him and that maybe his heart had gone out to him. For whatever reason, Jesus had not stopped earlier to heal him. But now here he was, in the most unusual of circumstances, lying in front of him. I think this would have delighted Jesus. And so what started with a moment of compassion, the picking up of a paralysed man, concluded with an act of faith and a life changed and healed.

If faith is the ligaments and sinews that hold the Body of Christ together, then compassion is the blood vessels that keep those ligaments and sinews alive and healthy. Compassion is the essential foundation for faith to be built upon. Compassion is about the heart. It is about the heart's longing for others to know God and for God to be made known. Compassion is our motivation and our strength. Without it, we are hard-hearted and will lack the persisting desire to see faith exercised; we will end up pursuing power. But compassion is also an unseen foundation, it is away from the crowd, it is unglamorous. It is unseen to all, that is, except Jesus who has an uncanny knack of recognizing it and turning it into world-changing faith. It may be that the crowd that had gathered in the house on that day went home remembering how a roof got broken through, that is the dramatic moment that lingers in the memory, but Jesus knew what had been done when no one else had been around. He had caught the aroma of compassion. Whenever we see dramatic exhibitions of faith, we should also expect to be able to look a little beneath the surface and discover the hallmark of authenticity that is compassion.

A quick examination of some of the people who have impacted the world for the sake of the Kingdom of God confirms the importance of compassion. Think of George Muller running his orphanage in Bristol. He never asked anybody for any money, he simply prayed that their needs would be met and they never went short. Remember William Wilberforce and his campaign to see slavery abolished. He put up with ridicule year after year until finally he saw it abolished just days before his own death. In our own day and age, think of Jackie Pullinger and her ministry to the lawless world of drug users in the walled city of Hong Kong. I once heard Jackie Pullinger say that the Church needed people who had soft hearts and hard feet if we were to be effective in our mission to the world. This statement accurately sums up the importance of compassion. Having soft hearts is about an expanding capacity to be moved by another's situation and having hard feet is about being prepared to go wherever we are called in order to see God's love melt the frosty grip of the enemy's hand. What these three people, as well as many others, demonstrate is that compassion is, and always has been, a vitally important element in our spiritual make-up that God is looking for in us, so that when he sees it he can bless the earth.

We have a number of terrific intercessors in our church and the thing that both confirms to me that they are gifted in this way and makes them effective in prayer is the way they feel so acutely the pain of the world. Strangely, this is a gift from God. It is not an easy one to live with, but the intense way that these intercessors empathize with the needs of the world, I believe, gives them a real cutting edge and a determination to see God move. Nowadays when some people receive this gift they wonder if there is something wrong with them. On a few occasions, people have asked me if I think they might be depressed because they have been so deeply affected by the needs of the world or by the situation of a friend. In the Middle Ages, this condition was better understood. It would have been more easily recognized that God sometimes allowed people to feel the weight of the world's needs, and that this was his way of calling people into the ministry of intercession. Compassion, you see, is crucial.

There is, however, a qualification to add to such a discussion on compassion: insensitive as it may seem to say it, not all acts of kindness are necessarily acts of compassion. There are many disabled people, for example, who feel that they have been reduced to being somebody else's project, that they have had things done to them or been taken somewhere with the best of intentions but without a great deal of consultation. It seems ungrateful to say it, but sometimes what was intended to be an act of compassion can turn out to be something rather more patronizing and even disempowering.

A friend who worked with us during our time in Nepal told us that he had been sent out on a wave of goodwill and prayer by his church in the USA when he first left for Nepal. He described how much love he thought he felt for the Nepali people and how good it was going to be to make such a difference to their needy country. The problem was that within a few weeks of arriving his family had had things stolen from their garden, they had been made to feel unwelcome by the visa department, they had been insulted in the bazaar and found learning the language a horrible struggle. He described how overnight he began to discover the love and compassion that he thought he had for Nepal and its people was evaporating in the hot and sticky conditions that exist just before the monsoon. In the end his time in Nepal was immensely fruitful. But the question remains: how can we tell the genuine article from a passing fraudulent feeling when it comes to compassion? Where does compassion come from and how is it sustained?

Psalm 103

This is a much loved psalm and a good place to start an exploration of the origins of compassion. It begins with the psalmist encouraging himself not to forget all the good things that God has done for him: 'Praise the LORD, O my soul, and forget not all his benefits'. The list of things that the psalmist goes on to rehearse seems to be a type of personal testimony. The implication is that the writer himself has been forgiven, healed, redeemed, crowned, satisfied and renewed. Just about every kind of adverse circumstance is listed as being an area of life in which God has profoundly worked. The question that we are longing to ask in the face of such overwhelming blessing is this: what has the psalmist done to deserve it? From verse 8 onwards we read the astonishing answer to this question. It begins with the words, 'The LORD is compassionate and gracious'. The writer of the psalm is well aware of his own sinfulness and that he has no right to expect any of God's goodness to be shown to him. He says that we may expect anger, but we do not get it: 'he does not treat us as our sins deserve'. When we read Psalm 103, we do not see a picture of God desperately trying to be patient with us, trying to stop himself erupting in rage, but a God whose whole basis for dealing with us is not anger but compassion. He is not trying to restrain his anger, he is simply not angry with us.

This is not an easy idea for us to get our heads round. Sometimes when we reflect on our lives and think about the bad things we believe ourselves to be guilty of, we want somebody to be angry with us because we feel that we deserve it. We may even feel that we have got away with something for too long. Inside we wish we had been caught and punished and therefore be able to move on with our lives, honestly able to say to the world, 'I know I did wrong but I faced up to what I did and now I'm going straight.' It can be a terrible thing to have some previous crime, sin or wrong still hanging over you, wondering every day if this will be the moment in history when all will be revealed. So, is God in his compassion indifferent to our sin? Does he just shrug his divine shoulders as if to say to us, 'Just forget it'? Fortunately he is not indifferent. He realizes that sins have a grip on us and seeks to separate them from us as far as the east is from the west (verse 12).

Verses 15–18 continue to develop the unexpected patterns of behaviour that God exhibits towards human beings. The psalmist speaks again from his own experience of the way God has treated him, which stands in complete contrast to the way human beings treat one another. The dominant characteristic of the world is that it is transitory. We are like dust and grass, easily blown from the face of the earth and forgotten. The dominant characteristic of God, however, is that his love is from everlasting to everlasting towards those who fear him. Here we come across an unexpected problem. We ought to be comforted by the fact that in the face of our finitude and mortality God says I will not let you simply sink into an abyss of nothingness. But to really accept the everlasting love of God we first have to accept the true state of our own selves. It is frankly deeply disturbing to meditate for too long on the fact that we are like dust and grass soon to be blown from the earth. These words are firmly etched in my memory because they are words I have used many, many times when taking funeral services. They are words, however, that put the whole of our lives into a very different context and should impact upon our priorities very significantly. To think about this for a while makes you wonder whether Jean Paul Sartre and the existentialist movement may not have been on to something when they spoke of the absence of God and the absence of meaning beyond what is meaningful for the individual. So we must think about these things.

We must resist the current temptation to think that Christian spirituality is about trying to convince ourselves that everything is really quite nice, and that by comparison with others we are really not that bad. Compassion is first cousin to prophecy. Truly compassionate action makes the statement that I am not going to abide by the law of a tooth for a tooth, or by the law that first asks the question, 'What's in this for me?', or has the attitude that seeks to bestow generosity as a means of cementing the status quo. An act of compassion makes very little sense. It evokes very different values. It does not follow convention. It has a very different understanding of the way our humanity is fostered.

It goes beyond being generous and points us to something altogether different, a new source of life, and in that sense it is prophetic. Psalm 103 is not one of those psalms that simply states that all is well with the world. It is a psalm that is from the heart of somebody who has lived a chequered life, who has been confronted not only with difficult external circumstances to endure, but also with his own inner addictions, compulsions and selfishness. He has faced how deeply undeserving he is of the love of God, but has nevertheless come to know the love of God reorienting his life and turning him, like a light-starved plant, back towards the sun.

Psalm 103 asserts that the key to understanding God is to understand and experience his steadfast love and compassion, to let his steadfast love and compassion get a grip on you. It is a psalm that started with the writer encouraging himself not to forget to praise God in his innermost being, and it ends with an invocation to the angels and to all the host of heaven to praise the Lord. The psalmist's reflection on compassion has truly put his existence into a different context. There has been the gift of inner freedom and renewal, but there has also been a new understanding of God and a new openness and availability to God's presence and power.

So compassion as we see it here is not about indifference to sin, it is not arbitrary kindness, it is not sentimentality. It starts with an understanding of our own acute need (not another's need) and then recognizes that we cannot resolve our own needs, our broken relationship with God, without attending to the needs of our neighbour. Compassion therefore has to do with putting aside our congenital desire to first decide whether or not somebody is worthy of our act of kindness and recognize that this process, a sort of dying to the self, is also a process that the Desert Fathers described as dying to our neighbour. Our awareness of our own need is there-fore crucial to our attempts to live compassionately. In fact, those moments of being excessively critical of another's life are very often the same moments when we most need to pay more attention to our own faults and, of course, are the moments when we are most reluctant to do so. Living com-passionately, living in a radically open way to God and to others, is the means of putting ourselves in the gulf stream of the life and love of God. This ruthless honesty about our-selves sounds, and is, a somewhat scary process and not at all what we imagined when we set out to live a compassionate life. However, when we can grasp all this, we discover that it is also a path to fulfilment for us as well, and then we dis-cover that it is also a means of making the Church's mission in the world more credible. Rowan Williams writes:

> A church that is living in such a way is the only church that will have anything different to say to the world; how deeply depressing if all the church offered were new and better ways to succeed at the expense of others, reinstating the scapegoat mechanisms that the cross of Christ should have exploded once and for all.[27]

The compassionate life, therefore, is about truth and mission: truth about ourselves and God, and mission to our neigh-bour. The very word *compassion* is a compound of two Latin words: *com* meaning with, and *passio* meaning to suffer. To suffer with someone is rather more of a commitment than being nice for a moment. In a way, I think the four friends who brought the paralysed man to Jesus in the story that I mentioned at the beginning of this chapter exhibited this sort of commitment. Their actions cost them something. They were soft-hearted but hard-footed. They were alongside the man in every practical way. They seemed to be with him beyond being physically close to him. They seemed to recognize something in Jesus and they wanted to connect the paralysed man to what they believed they had seen. It was an episode that was as much about them as it was about the person they were carrying. They needed to do this for their own spiritual growth. I do not mean that they had an unhealthy need to be needed, but that somehow it dawned upon them that their own journey of faith was inescapably tied up with the life and future of this paralysed man. They were all in it together. For compassion to flourish, a similar moment of enlightenment is required wherever there is need. Our own journey of faith is tied up with the life and future of the homeless, the refugee, the unemployed, the sick and the disabled.

This is the attitude of heart and mind that recognizes that we all need to go well beyond being nice to one another and acknowledges that we genuinely do need one another. In one sense, it was the paralysed man who brought these other four men into the life-changing presence of Jesus and not the other way around. Had the four of them gone to the Jesus meeting without the man and his now-famous mat, they might have sat in the front row but, I would suggest, they would not have got so close to Jesus; they would have experienced his power, but they would not have realized their faith potential. They would have been in Jesus' divine presence in a quite different, and probably not as significant, way. Similarly, we need those with disabilities around us in our churches and communities. When we stop and recognize this we also discover that our journey of faith is bound up with theirs. The presence of people with disabilities helps us see and experience the world and God differently and,

I would contend, more profoundly. This is not an attempt to dumb down the contribution of people with disabilities or to make out that their role is to be confined to shaping the attitudes of the rest of us. It is genuinely to assert that we need one another; we need to suffer with one another, rejoice with one another, celebrate with one another. And the key word here is *with*.

On a recent holiday to France we stayed in the atmospheric town of Beaune in the heart of Burgundy. The countryside all around the town consists of vineyards stretching away to the horizon as far as the eye can see. I knew of the famous wine produced on the gentle hills around Beaune before I arrived there. What I did not know about was the famous medieval hospital situated right in the heart of the town with its beautiful roof made of coloured tiles and its delicate wooden spire. It was originally built in 1443 by the Duke of Burgundy when the region was suffering badly from severe poverty as a result of the Hundred Years War. The Duke's intention was to build a 'palace for the poor' and so the very best of technology, design and craftsmanship went into its construction. In every respect it became a place that far exceeded minimum standards of care. It was also a place not only for those who were physically sick and dying but also, uniquely, for those who were poor in spirit, the discouraged, who needed some respite from the grinding poverty of everyday life. Its work obviously inspired others and it attracted donations and benefactors from further afield so that its work could be extended.

However, in Beaune the hospital was given the title '*Hôtel Dieu*', or 'God's Hotel', and this is a wonderfully evocative name. It is, of course, the custom in France to refer to a community's town hall as the *hôtel de ville*, and so it may have seemed natural in 1443 to include the word *hôtel* in the title of Beaune's new hospital. Nevertheless, the idea of this inspirational place of healing and care being known as God's Hotel, the place where he is, the place where he offers hospitality to those most in need, must also have been a vivid statement in fifteenth-century France, which, despite the existence of various charitable institutions, was still a feudal medieval society. It is interesting to speculate on what motivated the Duke of Burgundy to build and endow the hospital, just as it is interesting to wonder what made the four friends stop and pick up the paralysed man. The Hôtel Dieu was still functioning as a hospital until 1971, and its presence now as a place visited by tourists still points to some fundamental aspects of compassion.

It points to the central notion of seeing a person before seeing a problem, and it signals a commitment to seeing the restoration of a person's dignity and inner spirit not just his or her physical body. It highlights the need to be able to put aside all judgementalism and all attitudes of superiority, which in turn demands rigorous self-evaluation; and it requires an ongoing empathy that must be continually renewed and never taken for granted. Only when these very challenging characteristics are present in an act of kindness can it begin to be described as sustainable compassion.

Organized compassion

The Hôtel Dieu in Beaune is a wonderful example of organized compassion. For over five hundred years it provided a place of healing and hope. Organized compassion, as undertaken today by aid agencies for example, is a very difficult thing to do well. One of the most frustrating aspects of the work that is undertaken by development agencies is that certain causes and diseases seem easily to attract financial help and others simply do not. Leprosy, traditionally, has attracted much better funding than tuberculosis, which has historically struggled. Work among children with learning disabilities attracts support but work among adults with the same conditions is harder to sustain. Ironically, compassion has recently become something of a competitive industry. In the aftermath of the Boxing Day tsunami of 2004, which devastated vast coastal regions in the Indian Ocean, aid agencies were criticized for failing to work together and for competing to do the most high-profile work. Emergency supplies of food, tents and medicines were all displayed along airport runways with the agencies' names and logos all pointing towards the television cameras. The need for impressive publicity material and the consequent ability to be able to appeal for more money in the future was partly responsible for this. And it could become a more serious problem in the future as aid agencies, particularly non-governmental organizations, compete for funding from similar sources and have greater running costs to sustain their own organizations. Organized compassion has become big business and operates in a very competitive environment. This, of course, is not confined to international relief work but equally affects much smaller operations such as small residential care establishments. The world of organized compassion is competitive and keeping a watchful eye on its original purpose and motivation can prove hard work.

There are, however, many people in organizations around the world who remain the only people offering hope and kindness to displaced and suffering people who are forgotten by the world and by the news organizations who decide which causes are worthy of our attention. Authentic compassion must have an organized dimension: otherwise it will simply lack the ability to make any impact on the huge problems of our world today. But it is also good to start practising compassion in small ways in our own communities and neighbourhoods.

The story of Lazarus

The account of the raising from the dead of Jesus' friend Lazarus in the Gospel of John is one of the two moments when we read that Jesus wept. Lazarus had been in his tomb for four days when Jesus arrived in Bethany, just two miles outside Jerusalem. Lazarus had two sisters, Mary and Martha, and they had been mourning the loss of their brother. When Jesus saw the scene, we read that he was deeply troubled and moved. The term is the same as the one that describes Jesus' mood just a short time later in the Garden of Gethsemane as he contemplated his own death. And so we read that Jesus wept. His actions were obviously unexpected and startling. When he asked for Lazarus' tomb to be opened, Martha advised him to stop because the smell would be too bad! But the tomb was opened and Jesus shouted loudly for his friend to come out. What followed must almost have been comic. Lazarus was bound tightly in strips of linen and must have been tottering and swaying dangerously as he made his way into the sunlight. But he was alive.

It was, however, the response of Jesus to the scene of mourning that sheds further light on a discussion of compassion. He was deeply troubled. He was moved. He wept. The text implies that Jesus is angry about the situation before him. He is affronted by what has happened. Death and the

Kingdom of God have collided at Bethany, and when Jesus calls Lazarus out of the tomb he is making it clear that there is only going to be one outcome. St John has placed this story directly before the farewell discourse and the passion narrative as a way of foreshadowing what is going to happen in the life of Jesus himself. Jesus' demonstration of compassion is inextricably tied to his feelings of anger and indignation. Compassion is seen to be a confrontational act. Again, this is not necessarily what we might have expected when we began to think about the compassionate life. At first glance, when we read that Jesus wept, we are tempted to conclude that he was simply sad. But the feeling is much deeper, much more profound.

Strong feelings, such as those exhibited by Jesus at Bethany, can be a little overwhelming. Such feelings might be unwelcome visitors at first. They are not to be confused with the impulsive, knee-jerk reactions of a person who has an excitable temperament. Rather, compassion as seen here in Jesus is the product of being deeply in touch with the heart and mind of God, with time spent, often in silence, in the presence of God. This is why a great many people from the contemplative tradition are also passionate about social action and community transformation. It is why the nineteenth-century evangelicals felt the same way.

Compassion is the unlikely blending of gentleness (the product of self-awareness) and tough, persevering directness (the product of attentiveness to the heart and mind of God). There are no shortcuts to being a compassionate person. It is the product of being worked on and moulded by the Holy Spirit.

7

Fulfilling our vocation to compassion

Hidden love

A soldier of the First World War was fatally wounded and is being comforted in his last moments by an army padre. The padre asks the dying soldier if there are any messages he would like him to pass on to anyone at home. The soldier mentioned his mother and father but then, to the surprise of the padre, asks if he would also pass a message of gratitude to the man who had taught him at Sunday school as a child. Tell him, the soldier said, that all he taught me during those classes has given me the strength to face these last moments of my life. When the war was ended the army padre did in fact visit the Sunday school teacher as he had been requested. He was now an old man but as he listened to what the padre said to him, his eyes filled with tears. God forgive me, he said, when the padre had finished speaking, God forgive me for doubting the value of those Sunday school classes. And he explained how for years he had wondered if he was doing any good at all, how he had been discouraged by seeing so little fruit from his work, how he had thought about giving up so often.

This story reminds me of the apocryphal parable that Jesus told about the sheep and the goats. How at the final judgement the sheep and the goats would be separated to the left and to the right on the basis of their ministry to Jesus himself in the form of the hungry, the thirsty, the stranger, the naked, the sick and the imprisoned. The surprising thing about this parable, and the point that Jesus is making, is that those who are invited to share in the inheritance of the Kingdom of God, those who had ministered to Jesus, had no idea of what they were doing or of the eternal significance of their actions. They say to the king: when did we do these things? We had no idea that we were serving you in this way. All this is a mystery to us! When did we see you hungry, or thirsty, or estranged, or naked, or imprisoned? And the king replies to them: truly I tell you, whatever you did for the least of these brothers and sisters of mine, you did for me.

The acts of compassion carried out by those who are welcomed into the Kingdom of God were not only hidden from others, they were hidden also from themselves. The Sunday school teacher, discouraged as he may often have been, was surely one of these people also. Unaware of the true significance of what he was doing, unable to see why his teaching mattered or what difference it made, he was finally blessed in his old age to know what God had accomplished through him.

I am reminded also of the many carers and volunteers who give enormous time and energy to running youth clubs, sports clubs and social events for children and young people with learning disabilities. These selfless individuals seem oblivious to the effects of their compassion; they seem unaware of just how important they are to the lives of so many families. They are the sort of people who may one day say: when were we compassionate? When did we do these things that you speak of? A mountaineer was once asked why he had climbed Everest. 'Because it was there,' was his matter-of-fact reply. The same might be said about truly compassionate people. They care because there is a mountain of need.

Dietrich Bonhoeffer wrote about the hiddenness of compassion. He observed the potential paradox between Jesus' injunction in Matthew 5.16 ('let your light shine before others, so that they may see your good works and give glory to your Father who is in heaven') and Matthew 6.1–4 ('Beware of practising your piety before others in order to be seen by them . . . But when you give alms, do not let your left hand know what your right hand is doing, so that . . . your Father who sees in secret will reward you'). Bonhoeffer wrote:

> The first question to ask is: from whom are we to hide the visibility of our discipleship? Certainly not from other men, for we are told to let them see our light. No. We are to hide it from *ourselves*. Our task is simply to keep on following, looking only to our Leader who goes on before, taking no notice of ourselves or of what we are doing. We must be unaware of our own righteousness and see it only in so far as we look to Jesus; then it will not seem extraordinary, but quite ordinary and natural. Thus we hide the visible from ourselves in obedience to the word of Jesus.[28]

Hiding the visibility of our discipleship from ourselves, however, is no easy task. Bonhoeffer goes on to explain what he means:

> All that the follower of Jesus has to do is to make sure that his obedience, following and love are entirely spontaneous and unpremeditated. If you do good, you must not let your

left hand know what your right hand is doing, you must be quite unconscious of it. Otherwise you are simply displaying your own virtue, and not that which has its source in Jesus Christ. Christ's virtue, the virtue of discipleship, can only be accomplished so long as you are entirely unconscious of what you are doing. The genuine work of love is always hidden work.[29]

Bonhoeffer articulates for me an important principle about the growth into compassionate living, namely that compassion for Christians is about copying Jesus. Acts and moments of kindness and mercy are done because Jesus would have done them. It may therefore not even cross the mind that a particular act is an act of compassion, it is simply obedience, and in that respect such deeds are truly hidden from the person who carries them out.

In an earlier chapter, I mentioned the work of Asha in the slums of Delhi, work pioneered by Dr Kiran and Freddy Martin. Kiran began her work among these desperately poor people because there was nothing else she could do. It was not a project that began with a five- or ten-year plan for slum renovation. It did not begin with a business plan. It began without any money and hardly any resources. It all started when Kiran, a paediatrician by background, simply sat under a tree with a small medical bag and invited mothers to bring their children to her for treatment and care. This is the spontaneity and hiddenness of which Bonhoeffer spoke, and which he himself practised. This is the unpremeditated love that conceals compassion even from the person who carries out the act. Although Asha is now a growing and very efficiently run organization, it retains these essential values of spontaneity and hiddenness that are immediately apparent and evidently a part of Asha's DNA.

Freedom

Catholic theologian Hans Küng echoes many of Bonhoeffer's thoughts. Through the acceptance of discipleship comes an awareness of grace and an initiation into the life of compassion. Through *metanoia*, which Küng prefers to translate as 'conversion' rather than 'repentance', God's new future is given to his people:

> Jesus expects a different, a new man: a radically changed awareness, a fundamentally different attitude, a completely new orientation in thought and action. Jesus expects no more and no less than a fundamental, *total orientation of a man's life towards God*: an undivided heart, in the last resort serving not two masters but one.[30]

Küng goes on to talk about the surprising discovery that we make about the will of God when our lives become totally orientated towards him.

> God's will does not waver. Nor can it be manipulated. From all that we have said hitherto, from the concrete requirements of Jesus himself, it should already have become clear that God wills nothing for himself, nothing for his own advantage, for his greater glory. God wills nothing but man's advantage, man's true greatness and his ultimate dignity. This then is God's will: *man's well-being*. From the first to the last page in the Bible, it is clear that God's will aims at man's well-being at all levels, aims at his definitive and comprehensive good: in biblical terms, at the salvation of man and men. God's will is a helpful, healing, liberating, saving will.[31]

Küng's writing is immediately stimulating. The notion that 'God wills nothing but man's advantage' quickly makes us ask, 'Can this really be true? Is that what the Bible actually says? Does this imply that God is out to indulge the more selfish excesses of human desire?' On the other hand, once we have paused for a moment, once we have digested what Küng is saying, maybe he is giving us a further principle on which to build not a life of hedonism, but a life of compassion. Having established that this is the will of God for human beings, Küng discusses the implications.

God's will, Hans Küng suggests, relativizes all traditions, institutions and hierarchies. What does he mean? He means that all human institutions, practices, regulations and dogmas exist to serve humanity. Service to people, says Küng, has priority over observance of the law. God's cause is not law, but people. 'Consequently we cannot take God and his will seriously without at the same time taking seriously man and his well-being.'[32]

This principle is, of course, at the heart of the dispute that Jesus had with the religious establishment of his day. After he and his disciples had picked some ears of corn on the Sabbath, and were challenged for so doing, he defiantly replied that the Sabbath was made for people and not people for the Sabbath. Jesus often began his sayings with the words, 'You have heard it said . . . but I say . . .'. Those three words, 'but I say', implied that Jesus had assumed authority to modify the Law of Moses in order to make it contribute to human betterment and freedom rather than as a means of perverting power. This understanding of compassion remains deeply challenging today. Wherever it is suggested that people should come before rules and institutions, there will always be other people who become very bothered and talk about how dangerous it can be to establish the wrong precedents. I can just imagine the teachers of the Law who confronted Jesus taking this line. 'Now we've had one healing on the Sabbath, everybody will want healing on the Sabbath. Where will it all end?' It is such an argument that has prevented more complete cancellation of debt in the developing world. Financial institutions, it was thought by some, could not be seen to be allowing some countries simply to evade their financial responsibilities. What true compassion is about, however, is the complete reverse. It is not about the evasion of responsibility, it is about the empowerment of people to live up to their responsibilities. It is about setting people free so that they can play responsible roles in their communities. It is not about creating dependency. When Hans Küng says that God wills nothing but humanity's advantage, this is the advantage that he is talking about: freedom from all that disempowers and dehumanizes, and this should always be the product of compassion.

Here again, Jesus not only carries out acts of compassion and teaches about the importance of compassion, he also demonstrates that the freedom which compassion brings must be understood as a freedom to serve. Individuals are not to be set free in order that they might live to the detriment of everybody else. Jesus, probably the most free person who has ever lived, exists completely for others. Being free to live a life of compassionate service is the ultimate form of freedom. Jesus, of course, also allowed other people to show him compassion: a group of obviously quite wealthy women met many of his material needs, another woman poured expensive perfume on his feet, Simon of Cyrene carried his cross, Joseph of Arimathea and Nicodemus took his body, wrapped it in cloths and buried him in a tomb. Compassion resulted in freedom for all these people, and others, to do the most important things in their lives, the things that in many ways defined their lives.

Acts of kindness, acts of charity, acts of compassion, call them what you will, put our lives in a new perspective and orientate us towards truth. That is why Jesus allowed people to show him compassion. The woman who poured perfume on his feet was criticized by some, but Jesus turned on her accusers and said that she had done a beautiful thing, an act that with hindsight would be seen as a prophetic gesture. Our acts of compassion, the way in which we come alongside those who may have disabilities, for example, really therefore need to be motivated in the last resort by a spontaneous desire to know the truth about ourselves and God's will for our lives, as much as by the desire to be helpful.

The Doctrine of Enough

The Doctrine of Enough was a phrase coined by Charles Handy in his book *The Hungry Spirit: Beyond Capitalism: A Quest for Purpose in the Modern World*. The ideology of the free market and of capitalism, Handy explains, has decisively demonstrated that it can improve society more effectively than any other known approach to economics. However, this does not mean that it can deliver everything that human beings long for, or that as a system it is without fault:

> Businesses live and die by the market. It is a wonderful discipline, giving out its automatic signals as to where shortages lie, or unused surpluses. It is, with its built-in incentives and penalties, a spur to invention and improvement, but many do die in the process. Even big corporations seldom live longer than forty years, or deserve to. But schools, hospitals and welfare agencies cannot be allowed to die when they are inefficient, because there might not be any others nearby to replace them.[33]

The point that Handy is making is that there are areas of life within society where the market place alone cannot guarantee

124

best outcomes. The market place has only one measure of success: money. Most of us do not want to live in a society where money is the only measure of success, the only measure of what is admirable or of what is good. Most of us do not want our value as human beings to be determined by the size of our pay cheque.

As one means of introducing some perspective into our lives, Handy suggests that we look at the Doctrine of Enough. It is a doctrine, he says, that can apply both to an individual and to an organization. To decide for yourself what you need or want is to enter into a genuine place of freedom from the norms of society which tries very hard to dictate an ever more expensive list of essentials to daily living. Once you have achieved what you consider to be enough, you are then at liberty to use the time or money that is left over in whatever creative way you choose. The difficulty, as Handy points out, is deciding on what is enough. It is also making sure that everybody has a genuine opportunity of achieving their own personal target of what, for them, constitutes enough.

In corporate terms, the Doctrine of Enough is about the recognition that growth can mean better rather than bigger. Handy gives an example from Japan where some domestic industries, such as petrol sales, have their prices rigorously controlled.

> Companies are forced to compete on service, not price, which is kept high. The result is that a visit to the service station in Japan is like a visit to a beauty parlour with attendants swarming all over the car . . . Many would prefer the Japanese way, which recognises that there can be proper limits to price competition in the interest of a decent society. Better, not richer.[34]

Handy's Doctrine of Enough does not undermine the benefits of the market economy. What it offers is another piece in the puzzle that ultimately forms a rounded picture of compassionate living. It is recognition that a consumer-driven society, left unchecked, will ultimately become bloated with excess and consume itself. Handy challenges the assumption that prosperity is an end in itself. He asks what is the point of generating wealth? 'The sobering thought', says Handy, 'is that individuals and societies are not, in the end, remembered for how they made their money, but for how they spent it.'[35] We may want to question whether or not human nature would ever truly be able to appropriate a Doctrine of Enough. History would be pessimistic. But Handy's ideas contain echoes of the Sermon on the Mount:

> 'Therefore I tell you [says Jesus], do not worry about your life, what you will eat or what you will drink, or about your body, what you will wear. Is not life more than food, and the body more than clothing? Look at the birds of the air; they neither sow nor reap nor gather into barns, and yet your heavenly Father feeds them. Are you not of more value then they? And can any of you by worrying add a single hour to your span of life? (Matthew 6.25–27)

What sort of person would we become if we were able to take this piece of the Sermon on the Mount to heart? Well, we might be someone that others would describe as care-free; we might be somebody who didn't take themselves too seriously, who spent more time listening than talking when in the company of others; we would probably be somebody who had precious little savings. We might buy our clothes in the sales or in charity shops, but do so with the inner confidence that made it appear that we had spent ten times the amount. We would probably be somebody who embraced the Doctrine of Enough. And we would also, I believe, have an unintentional compassion for people, a natural empathy with others, which stemmed from the security of knowing that our daily needs, our identity needs and our need for belonging came first and foremost from our Father in heaven. It is, in fact, virtually impossible to live an externally compassionate life when just below the surface we haven't even begun to participate in, or experience, the abundant life that God has prepared for those who seriously trust him.

Before we think that all this is far too difficult, that we have far too much to let go of, far too much to learn, listen again to what Jesus says. All this, he makes clear, is to be received as gift. Again this is not what we expect. We imagine that our task is to accumulate, to store up enough wealth so that we have plenty of spare to give away to others. This sort of philanthropy is undoubtedly a good thing, but most of us will never be in a position to become serial philanthropists on a grand scale. So what are we to do? The good news is that the principle established here by Jesus is that once we have come to see that everything we have is from God, whether that is a little or a lot, that the stuff we have in our homes and bank balances is given as a gift, we do not need to compare ourselves to others. In fact, many of the most compassionate people I have met have also been some of the poorest I have met, or they have been people struggling with their mental health. Some have even been struggling with drug addictions.

So a large fortune is not the main qualification for compassionate living. Handy's Doctrine of Enough asks questions of the spiritual life too. One of the difficult things to balance in the spiritual life is the universal Christian vocation to live with what we have been given, to be content with what we have, to live an ordinary life well, with the equally scriptural injunction to strive for more, to know more of God, to remain spiritually hungry. Another way of articulating this tension is to ask how we are supposed to hold together the knowledge that we should live in simplicity with the knowledge that God wants to bless us beyond our wildest dreams. It is no easy task. Failure to hold these things together has led the Church at times into teaching a very unattractive form of prosperity gospel, on the one hand (which disdains the poor), and a sterile rejection of all things material or beautiful, at the other extreme (which seems to make an idol of poverty). Neither of these two extremes can ever create an environment in which a life of compassion can flourish. Maybe the secret of avoiding these extremes, of embracing life as a gift, is not to wait until you feel a compassionate impulse prompting you into action, but simply to do something compassionate now. Maybe we need to borrow a phrase from the world of psychotherapy, modify it slightly for our purposes, and engage in what could then be termed 'cognitive behavioural spirituality'. As has been said elsewhere in this book, sometimes doing the right thing (orthopraxis) comes before understanding things correctly (orthodoxy). This, after all, seemed to be the pattern that Jesus established for his own apprentices.

Vulnerability

Finally, I want to talk about vulnerability. Many of the disabled people I have met have been vulnerable and they have taught me just how important it is to acknowledge that I too am vulnerable. When you are given a particular position or a particular responsibility it is so very easy to think that those around you are wanting you to be virtually omnipotent and so that is what you try to be. Attempted Omnipotence is exhibited by a range of people, probably most of us at some point in our lives, from those seeking (admirably) to be good parents to those with big salaried jobs like chief executive officers. It is well known that Attempted Omnipotence is both disempowering for anyone close to you, as you try and do everything, as well as being a way of achieving meltdown for yourself. Vulnerability is usually learned the hard way, but however it is learned, it is another thing that is essential to fulfilling a vocation to compassionate living.

It should quickly be pointed out that vulnerability and incompetence are not the same thing at all, although they are often mistaken as twins. We think that if we admit to being vulnerable others may conclude that we are incompetent. Children, employees, parishioners or whoever are entitled to expect commitment and competence from parents, employers and priests, but these things without vulnerability lead inevitably towards self-righteousness, inflexible dogmatism, hardness of heart and deadly legalism. Learning vulnerability was a lesson that the apostle Peter found very hard to accept and, even now, the reinstatement of Peter after he had denied Jesus is painful to read. Paul wrote honestly about his thorn in the flesh, Mary the mother of Jesus was very frightened and, in the Old Testament, many prominent characters such as Moses, Elisha, Joseph, Gideon, Miriam and Samson, to name but a few, all had to come to terms with vulnerability. The encouraging news is that they did it and so can we!

The award-winning book *Fearfully and Wonderfully Made*, by Philip Yancey and Dr Paul Brand, talks about the spiritual lessons we can learn from our bodies and the body's different functions. It is a wonderful reflection on Dr Brand's lifetime of work as one of the world's leading specialists on leprosy. There is a chapter on the importance of the skeleton which, Dr Brand reflects, acts like truth in our lives. If it is going to be of any use it has to be strong and consistent and tough. When a bone is broken, we find we cannot move our bodies properly and we cannot bear weight. Dr Brand goes on to point out that as humans, we are supported by an interior skeleton and that this again is how truth should function for us. It is something that gives us inner strength.

He then compares the human skeleton with that of a crayfish, which has an exterior skeleton. This exterior skeleton takes the form of a hard outer shell that offers protection from predators and provides something firm against which the crayfish's muscles can act. However, this exoskeleton also means that the crayfish has only a short period each year in which it can grow. Once a year the crayfish undergoes a ritual of contorted wriggling and anguished struggle during which it carefully sheds its old shell. It is not unusual for limbs or antennae to get damaged during this process and once it is completed the exhausted crayfish is intensely vulnerable without its hard shell for protection. For the next few weeks it is able to grow until its new exoskeleton hardens around it like a straitjacket and once again its body is locked inside a hard, tight-fitting, crusty box.

Philip Yancey and Dr Brand comment on the lessons learned:

> I have undergone a parallel process of Christian moulting. I started in a close-knit group holding rigid ideas of what a Christian was and who was worthy of fellowship. As I

travelled and gained breadth of experience, I realised that not all Christians were of my race with my style of worship and my footnoted doctrinal statement. So I grew a new shell, until my next experience came along. I tended to lapse into seeing the Christian family as an exclusive set of *people like me* encased in a shell. Inside, all was warm and comfortable; outside, the shell protected us from 'the world.'

But never did Jesus describe anything resembling an exoskeleton that would define all Christians. He kept pointing to higher, more lofty demands, using words like love and joy and fullness of life – internal words. When someone came to him for a specific interpretation of an Old Testament rule, usually he pointed instead to the principle behind it.

Jesus understood that rules and governing behaviour are meant to free movement and promote growth as a vertebrate skeleton does, not to inhibit growth as an exoskeleton does.[36]

If we are to become more compassionate, we have to avoid wearing our skeletons on the outside. It might mean vulnerability. It might mean that some of our most treasured dogmas and religious habits have to be forensically examined for any trace of legalism and self-righteous piety, because these were the things that aroused most condemnation from the mouth of Jesus. As I have said, it has very often been people with disabilities that have taught me the most about vulnerability. Every other year, our church has a weekend away to the South Devon coast. On these occasions, we try to organize a small team of people to come and help lead our children's and youth work. We have been blessed with some wonderful people over the years. On our most recent visit to Sidmouth, we were able to take with us a young youth worker called Ed who has cerebral palsy. We only had a small number of our youth group with us but I was immediately impressed by the relationship that Ed developed with them. Ed's obvious passion for youth work and for God was apparent straightaway. The young people did not bat an eyelid at having to push their leader's wheelchair if they went out for walks, or even, on a couple of occasions, when they needed to cut up Ed's food. Here was somebody making themselves vulnerable to serve others. In one sense Ed was regarded just like any other youth leader would be regarded, which was how it should have been. He was the youth leader first and foremost. Being a person with cerebral palsy came a distant second. The fact of cerebral palsy was about as relevant as the colour of his hair. And yet I suspect that his impact upon the group went well beyond the things he taught them from the Bible, simply because he allowed the group to serve and help him as well as him teaching and helping them to grow in their faith. They were all in something together.

When we allow God to soften our hearts, to take off our tough exoskeletons, to fulfil his purpose in our lives, we can discover that there is truth in the saying of Jesus that those who lose their lives for his sake will in the end find real life. But we cannot have it both ways. We cannot know real life while hiding behind the various dogmatic and institutional shells of our own creation. The vocation to the compassionate life is a sister to the vocation of the peace-maker and the vocation of the Christian witness. They are all to be universally embraced by those who aspire to Christian discipleship. The compassion and the hope that we are called to demonstrate is not a product of human ingenuity or good intention or liberal democracy. It is a characteristic of God that he makes available to us in Jesus. There is in our world so much tension between people of different races and religions; so much fear generated by the unequal spread of wealth; so much anxiety caused by the uncertainty of climate change and the exhaustion of natural resources. There is in our neighbourhoods so much pain and frustration caused by the breakdown of relationships, narrow-minded parochialism and self-interest. It would be easy to get depressed and cynical. Where do we see signs of hope? We see signs of hope where we see compassion demonstrated by people stopping for another in need. Where this happens we see something that we instinctively know has enhanced our humanity. Compassion of this nature can be expressed in the workplace both by an employer towards an employee and vice versa; it can be expressed between neighbours; it can be expressed between countries or between religious groups. It can be expressed institutionally, in the values an organization aspires to, and it can be expressed spontaneously if we are prepared to live vulnerably without an exoskeleton. Compassion is what our world needs. It is also what God offers.

Fear, suspicion, insecurity and selfishness are ultimately spiritual problems that require a spiritual answer. The way of Jesus was and is not simply to offer advice or philosophy from afar, but to offer himself. He even goes beyond the offer of practical compassion, and extends personal compassion. We see in Jesus not simply acts of kindness but a direct challenge to, and ultimately a victory over, the forces of evil that make the world hard, cold, angry, prejudiced and violent. When we participate in this activity of the Kingdom of God, this life of compassion, we are not simply involved in perpetuating acts of kindness. We are in fact involved in the process of God's Kingdom coming on earth, creating an environment in which faith in Jesus can grow, and challenging evil. Such a vocation can be frightening as we discover new things about ourselves, but life-changing too as the beauty of God pours out of us through the cracks in our lives and we discover that to stop for others, to listen to others, to live for others defines our existence and makes us whole.

Notes

1 Melvyn Matthews, *Both Alike to Thee* (SPCK 2000), p. 37.
2 Jürgen Moltmann, *The Crucified God* (SCM Press 1989), p. 47.
3 Moltmann, *The Crucified God*, p. 48.
4 Philip Yancey, *Disappointment with God* (Zondervan 1988), p. 58.
5 Sally Vickers, *Mr Golightly's Holiday* (Harper Perennial 2003), p. 117.
6 Amanda Shao Tan, 'The disabled Christ', *Transformation*, vol. 15, no. 4 (1998).
7 Karl Barth, *Dogmatics in Outline* (SCM Press 1949).
8 Nancy Eiesland, *The Disabled God* (Abingdon Press 1994), p. 66.
9 Eiesland, *The Disabled God*, p. 75.
10 David Adam, *The Wisdom of St Augustine* (Lion 1997).
11 NTs, or neurologically typical, is the term given to people who are not on the autistic spectrum by the (self-styled) Aspies (those with Asperger's syndrome). See Michael Blastland, *Joe: The Only Boy in the World* (Profile Books 2006).
12 Walter Brueggemann, *Genesis* (John Knox Press 1982), p. 25.
13 Brueggemann, *Genesis*, p. 25.
14 John O'Donahue, *Beauty* (Perennial 2005), p. 6.
15 Jean Vanier, *Becoming Human* (Darton, Longman & Todd 1998), p. 46.
16 Rowan Williams, *Lost Icons* (Morehouse Publishing 2000), p. 58.
17 Williams, *Lost Icons*, p. 61.
18 Brueggemann, *Genesis*, p. 53.

19 Blastland, *Joe*, p. 103.

20 David J. A. Clines, *The Theme of the Pentateuch* (JSOT Press 1978), p. 65.

21 Philip Yancey, *Disappointment with God*, p. 116.

22 David Runcorn, *Christ, Desire and the Will of God* (SPCK 2003), p. 53.

23 Henri J. M. Nouwen, *Here and Now* (Darton, Longman & Todd 1994), p. 65.

24 From an article in *The Merton Journal*, vol. 11, no. 1 (Easter 2004), p. 30.

25 Dallas Willard, *The Divine Conspiracy* (Fount 1998), p. 414.

26 Taken from a taped address given by Thomas Merton to novices at Gethsemani.

27 Rowan Williams, *Silence and Honey Cakes* (Lion 2003), p. 34.

28 Dietrich Bonhoeffer, *The Cost of Discipleship* (SCM Press 1990), p. 142.

29 Bonhoeffer, *The Cost of Discipleship*, p. 143.

30 Hans Küng, *On Being a Christian* (Collins 1976), p. 249.

31 Küng, *On Being a Christian*, p. 251.

32 Küng, *On Being a Christian*, p. 254.

33 Charles Handy, *The Hungry Spirit* (Arrow Books 1998), p. 17.

34 Handy, *The Hungry Spirit*, p. 115.

35 Handy, *The Hungry Spirit*, p. 127.

36 Philip Yancey and Dr Paul Brand, *Fearfully and Wonderfully Made* (Zondervan 1987), p. 109.